DRINK

in the

SUMMER

Our Lives: Diary, Memoir, and Letters

Social history contests the construction of the past as the story of elites—a grand narrative dedicated to the actions of those in power. Our Lives seeks instead to make available voices from the past that might otherwise remain unheard. By foregrounding the experience of ordinary individuals, the series aims to demonstrate that history is ultimately the story of our lives, lives constituted in part by our response to the issues and events of the era into which we are born. Many of the voices in the series thus speak in the context of political and social events of the sort about which historians have traditionally written. What they have to say fills in the details, creating a richly varied portrait that celebrates the concrete, allowing broader historical settings to emerge between the lines. The series invites materials that are engagingly written and that contribute in some way to our understanding of the relationship between the individual and the collective. Manuscripts that include an introduction or epilogue that contextualizes the primary materials and reflects on their significance will be preferred.

SERIES TITLES

A Very Capable Life: The Autobiography of Zarah Petri · John Leigh Walters

Letters from the Lost: A Memoir of Discovery · Helen Waldstein Wilkes

A Woman of Valour: The Biography of Marie-Louise Bouchard Labelle · Claire Trépanier

Man Proposes, God Disposes: Recollections of a French Pioneer · Pierre Maturié, translated by Vivien Bosley

Xwelíqwiya: The Life of a Stó:lō Matriarch · Rena Point Bolton and Richard Daly

Mission Life in Cree-Ojibwe Country: Memories of a Mother and Son · Elizabeth Bingham Young and E. Ryerson Young, edited and with introductions by Jennifer S.H. Brown

Rocks in the Water, Rocks in the Sun · Vilmond Joegodson Déralciné and Paul Jackson

The Teacher and the Superintendent: Native Schooling in the Alaskan Interior, 1904–1918 · Compiled and annotated by George E. Boulter II and Barbara Grigor-Taylor

Leaving Iran: Between Migration and Exile · Farideh Goldin

Amma's Daughters: A Memoir · Meenal Shrivastava

Under the Nakba Tree: Fragments of a Palestinian Family in Canada · Mowafa Said Househ

Drink in the Summer: A Memoir of Croatia · Tony Fabijančić

A MEMOIR OF CROATIA

Drink
in the
Summer

TONY FABIJANČIĆ

◊ AU PRESS

Published by AU Press, Athabasca University
1 University Drive, Athabasca, Alberta T9S 3A3
https://doi.org/10.15215/aupress/9781771993807.01

Cover design by David Fassett / Notch Design
Cover photograph by Tony Fabijančić, texture images by raw pixel:
5975965, 2368477, 2896223
Interior photographs by Tony Fabijančić unless otherwise indicated.
Interior design by Natalie Olsen / Kisscut Design
Printed and bound in Canada

Library and Archives Canada Cataloguing in Publication
Title: Drink in the summer : a memoir of Croatia / Tony Fabijančić.
Names: Fabijančić, Tony, 1966– author.
Series: Our lives—diary, memoir, and letters.
Description: Series statement: Our lives—diary, memoir, and letters |
Includes bibliographical references.
Identifiers: Canadiana (print) 20230457355 | Canadiana (ebook)
20230457371 | ISBN 9781771993807 (softcover) | ISBN 9781771993821
(EPUB) | ISBN 9781771993814 (PDF)
Subjects: LCSH: Fabijančić, Tony, 1966– —Travel—Croatia. | LCSH:
Croatia—Description and travel. | LCSH: Croatia—Biography. | LCGFT:
Autobiographies.
Classification: LCC DR1517 .F33 2023 | DDC 914.97204/3—DC23

We acknowledge the financial support of the Government of Canada
through the Canada Book Fund (CBF) for our publishing activities and the
assistance provided by the Government of Alberta through the Alberta
Media Fund.

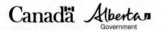

Contents

Preface

Quite a few years ago, this book started as an ambitious scholarly project on cold- and warm-water islands, around a dozen of them, which in time got chiselled down to a book of travels to the Croatian islands.

Although I went on to finish a manuscript, some comments by an early reader, Pamela Holway, made me see that my book hadn't yet emerged into its final form. I realized I had much to say about my half century in the north of Croatia, especially about the village and the surrounding valleys where I spent my formative years in Yugoslavia, a country that no longer exists. My story about the islands, I saw, was always folded into my life in the north, from where every journey to the sea began.

Two worlds—the continental interior of green valleys and plum orchards on the one hand, and the austere and skeletal karst coast on the other—were the two halves of my Croatian life. Each world wasn't just a different geographical landscape, but a different emotional and psychological one. The first felt like home; the other always seemed unfamiliar and new. In the north were family and friends who helped shape the social part of my character, but in the south I was an anonymous stranger, and while one was steeped with my own history and freighted with time, the other existed mainly in the present of my travelling. Yet both halves of my Croatia were connected also. In both, I had physical adventures, tests of the body. In each, I was always on the move, always travelling, exhibiting the restless instincts of my migratory family. In writing, I used similar techniques throughout. I balanced the open confessional nature of memoir with the reticence and mystery of literary fiction (because I felt that readers should sometimes be invited to make up their own minds). I adopted both a relaxed, conversational, digressive register that was in keeping with all those conversations in kitchens over *gemišt* and a tighter, journalistic, less demotic one. The result is a memoir, not a comprehensive historical, sociological, political or anthropological analysis of Yugoslavia and Croatia.

The village of Srebrnjak is a string of houses fifteen kilometres southwest of Zagreb. More hamlet than village, it was a community of peasants in the early 1970s, which turned into a white-collar weekend retreat and country "suburbia" where most of the vineyards had disappeared and no one farmed anymore. With these larger societal changes came my own— from childhood, youth, and young manhood to middle age and after. I got to know many villagers very well. I learned about their stories, the practices of their working days, and the often haunting, all-too-human saga of their lives. I knew the seasons in Srebrnjak too, the profusions of spring and summer, and the cold, spectral fall and winter.

By contrast, in all my years travelling to the Croatian islands it was always summer; a cold *bura* didn't blow from the mountainous hinterland and the towns weren't silent and desolate as they are in the winter. I walked in the hottest conditions, swam off remote beaches and islets in hidden coves. And even though I had set routines at work and at home, on the islands I broke free, shrugged off the prim atmosphere and little orthodoxies of academia and shed my former self the farther south I travelled and the farther offshore I went. Like so many Croatians every summer, like the millions of others who left behind their own drizzly north for the sun and blue sea, I too escaped to the islands in the south. Yes, the Croatian islands have a long history, and are long inhabited, but to me they were always places of discovery and liberation, of new beginnings.

Acknowledgements

From 1969 on, my father took us to what was then still Yugo-slavia and, through his own drive to go home, sparked my interest in Croatia for the rest of my life. In later years, while working on this book, I also travelled with him to some of the islands and had long talks about the past. My son, Lucas, stuck it out with the two of us, even though our trips were event-ful in the wrong ways at times, and probably too uneventful at others. My wife shared her memories of her youth in Yugoslavia, applied her cogent editorial skills to parts of the book and set me right, as she always does, on all my mis-takes. Numerous chapters were edited by my mother, Ursula Fabijančić, who offered several poignant memories. Thank you to Renata Schellenberg for generously going over an early ver-sion of the manuscript and to Robyn Anderson for scanning slides and old photographs. Thanks also to Denise Fabijančić, Natasha Fabijančić, Pamela Holway, Tonček Juranko, Peter Midgley, Lois Sherlow, and Goran Vojković for their sugges-tions and commentary. Finally, I want to recognize my family in Croatia for taking me into their homes year after year, for which I can never adequately repay them.

Note on Pronunciation

The Croatian language is written in a modified version of the Latin alphabet originally developed by the Croatian linguist Ljudevit Gaj. For the most part, Latin letters are pronounced as they are in English, but readers should note the following:

c—*ts*, as in ca*ts*
č—*ch*, as in *ch*ur*ch*
ć—like *ch*, but softer, as in fu*t*ure
đ—like *dj*, as in Geor*g*e
e—as in s*ay*
j—*y*, as in *y*esterday
š—*sh*, as in *sh*ip
ž—*zh*, as in trea*s*ure

DRINK

in the

SUMMER

When the Sea Is Bluer + Brač

"Like a horse back to its stable" was how my mother put it. My father hadn't been to Yugoslavia since his escape in 1963 so he was eager to return to Srebrnjak, the village of his birth. It was 1969. The three of us had been in France, near Montpellier, where my mother was finishing her doctorate in French literature. He had bought a new white Citroën DS 21 Palas, the car he would later ship to New York on the ss *Michelangelo* and then drive to Alberta in the winter of 1971. We arrived in Srebrnjak late at night when everyone in the house was asleep. It was raining and muddy and when they were awakened, my mother said, the people looked like a primitive bunch, smelling of the stable. The house had an odour of dank concrete and sour milk and had only one light, which meant we had to go to our bedroom upstairs by candlelight, so my mother was disappointed because my father's descriptions of Srebrnjak didn't match her first experience of the place itself.

The next day everything was different, she recalled. The grass was green and shiny from the rain, the sun had come out, the trees were heavy with plums and apples, and the people seemed so friendly. So hardworking, so kind to her.

What a difference! Her mood improved from then on. They cooked for us and washed our clothes by hand using water from the well, which freed her of those chores and gave her more time to study. And she didn't let the inconvenience of the outhouse, located at the end of a narrow corridor between the pig sties and cow stable, spoil the trip for her.

I had memories of this time, which became the stories my mother told me. I chased chickens in the yard and played with two girls who lived next door, Milena and Zdenka. I learned my first Croatian from them and spoke about myself in the *ženski rod*, the feminine gender, my mother said with a laugh. I had other memories that were entirely my own. When we came home late at night from somewhere, travelling on the pitch-black Srebrnjak road, the car's headlights lit up the glowing eyes of creatures in the bushes and shone on the white trunks of trees. White eyes and white trees in the sleepy blackness. At some point I figured out that the eyes were those of foxes or cats and the trees were plum trees that had been painted with lime to protect them against rabbits and insects and also to reflect the glare of the spring sun and slow the growth of blossoms when a late frost could kill them.

My memories began in earnest in 1977. I was eleven years old, and I remember flying into Zagreb and seeing the orange-tiled roofs of the houses among the hills, the hills that looked like a carpet bunched up and tied together with grey strings that were the roads. I don't remember the drive from the airport. However, Srebrnjak stayed with me from the beginning. On each side of the gravel road, which was full of holes and had no streetlights, there were houses of brick with roofs of the same orange tiles I'd seen from the plane, mounds of manure behind the barns, and chickens, ducks and turkeys wandering around dirt yards. Some yards were closed off by iron gates from behind which mangy, unfriendly dogs on chains barked at us as we passed. Narrow bands of wheat and corn went all the way to the top of the hills on each side of the valley.

We arrived at the house where we were going to spend the summer. Located on the left upper part of Srebrnjak, it was a two-storey concrete and brick building set back fifty metres from the road, with a field of cut grass in front, plum and apple trees behind, and a long barn of dark wood and concrete blocks on the right. Chickens and turkeys roamed in the open yard. On the hill were two vineyards. The whole place gave me an airy and wholesome feeling from the start.

The woman who owned the land was Strina Slava ("Aunt" Slava). An important figure in my father's life, though I didn't know this in 1977, she had assumed care of him and his two brothers after the death of their father, Josip, in 1943 when he was serving with the Hrvatsko domobranstvo, the Croatian Home Guard, during the Second World War, and after my father's mother abandoned the boys four years later to marry a man across the hill.[1] When Strina Slava's husband, my father's uncle, died soon after of tuberculosis, she became responsible for six kids—my father and his siblings, as well as her own three daughters.

They lived, all of them, in a wooden house part way up the hill. Inside was only a kitchen and a bedroom and they slept in those two rooms. "A lot of us crammed together," my father remembered. "But it kept us warm in the winter! We had bunks that pulled out from under the beds, and some

---

[1] The Domobrani, as members of the Croatian Home Guard were known, served as the regular army of the Independent State of Croatia (NDH, for Nezavisna država Hrvatska). The NDH was established in April 1941 shortly after the fall of Yugoslavia to the Axis powers. The NDH was founded and governed by the Ustaše, a fascist Croatian nationalist movement, but with the backing of Nazi Germany and the Italian fascists. The Domobrani operated in conjunction with the Ustaša Militia but remained separate from it until late 1944, when the two were amalgamated. Despite the relationship between the Domobrani and the fascist Ustaše, my grandfather, like most peasants of his place and time, was first and foremost a patriotic Croat.

of us slept in the kitchen." During the hot months he and his brothers spent their nights in the hay loft of the barn. There was an outhouse, but in the summer he relieved himself outside. "I used two or three leaves to wipe my ass!" They took baths in a barrel that was filled with hot water off the wood stove; kids first, adults last. Because his family was poor, there wasn't much to eat in the years after the war. "A lot of beans, a lot of potatoes, a lot of fucking *žganci*! Corn meal and pork grease every day, and meat only on Sundays!" As a result, he acquired the habit of eating fast, which is why to this day he always finishes before the rest of us, but it's also why he enjoys cooking fine meals, taking his time and savouring the experience, drinking wine as he goes along, overdoing it with all the spices and herbs, his haute cuisine. . . .

A typical peasant woman, Strina Slava in 1977 was small and plump and wore a kerchief knotted at the back of her neck and an apron over her dark skirt. She lived in the new house with one of her three daughters and her daughter's husband, and even though the land was legally hers, she didn't seem in charge of anything anymore. While we ate at the table, she sat on the box by the wood stove, either eating from the plate in her lap or waiting for us to finish before she went to the table and had her almost surreptitious, guilty meal.

Strina Slava was nice to me, always smiled when she saw me, and showed me where the apples were in the cellar. I used to follow her around the yard. One time, I still remember it, she caught hold of a chicken and went with it behind the barn. I peeked around the side and saw her holding the squawking fluttering body and doing something to it. I knew, but didn't know, what she was doing. A weird feeling filled me. Strina, who was a shy and gentle woman, had no problems cutting the head off a chicken. And yet I can remember her feeling pity for some of the animals too, like for the pigs that had been castrated without anaesthetic and that afterwards were let out in the yard to recover and to feed.

If I spent time with Strina Slava and developed a closeness to her, her son-in-law, Štefek Juranko, was the most removed from my memory. He was a distant figure I saw cleaning out the cow dung in the barn or scything grass in the evenings with a wicker basket on his back. As far as I can remember, he never addressed me. I don't think he had patience or time for kids. I was just the son of my father; that was about it. He was a lean, handsome man of medium height, clean-shaven, with a hooked nose and sharp eyes. He always wore a cap, except for meals. The Štefek I saw spent most of his life working around the place, though I know now he also had a job at an aluminum factory, called *Top*, in Kerestinec, and had to walk the three kilometres there and back. In later years rode a bicycle. Like many Yugoslavs, he was a factory worker in the mornings, a peasant in the afternoons and evenings. I didn't see him socialize much at the kitchen table after a meal or relax outside the house during the summer, as his wife Mila did (Strina Slava's daughter and my father's cousin).

FIGURE 1. Strina Slava, 1977. Photograph by Ursula Fabijančić.

FIGURE 2. Štefek Juranko, with sister-in-law, Draga, 1977. Photograph by Ursula Fabijančić.

FIGURE 3. Tony Fabijančić on the crest of the Srebrnjak hill, 1977. Photograph by Ursula Fabijančić.

Mila in those years was a thin, gristly woman with a sarcastic laugh who would pinch me on the cheek with her strong, chapped hands as a show of affection, which hurt and which I dreaded. Her lively mind and dry sense of humour eventually made her an interesting and central figure in my life in Srebrnjak, and I see now that her personality had a lasting impact on my father. But in 1977 I noticed only her physical self. I saw her cook, work in the garden, clean the pigsties and milk the cows. She always walked slowly towards the barn, in no rush to get there. She trudged even more slowly up the hill to the cornfield for an afternoon of hoeing. If there was any resentment about the direction her life had gone, there was to me no hint of it other than her body language; it would take many years for me to get a fuller picture of Mila's attitude, and that only near the very end.

I spent much of my time running around the place. I ran through the family's two vineyards, and I ran on top of the hill, from where I could see the orange roofs of Srebrnjak and the shimmering white dots in the distance: Zagreb. Then I ran back down again for a drink of cool well water from the steel pail that sat on a stool in a side room. Whenever I was on the hilltop, I noticed how quiet it was. Just the wind in the branches and an occasional rooster crowing in the valley. If I was in the cornfield, hiding out from everyone and spying on the goings-on below, I could hear the stalks rustling. That was all.

I wore overalls or black lederhosen that my maternal grandmother had brought back from Germany the year before, and a racoon hat I soon ditched because of the heat. The bowie knife I wanted to bring with me on the plane was confiscated by airport security for some reason. I imagined myself a combination of Davy Crockett and Aragorn from *The Lord of the Rings*.

A precocious reader, I'd already finished *The Lord of the Rings* the summer before, reading for hours on the front steps of my grandparents' house in west Edmonton in the blue afternoon shade of the big spruces my grandfather had planted. That world arrived in Srebrnjak in the person of my grandmother,

Helene Kristine Luise Panzer (née Bartschek), who visited Yugoslavia in 1977. I still find it strange to imagine her transported from her Crestwood home, where she had become a permanent fixture for me, like the house itself. However, there is a photo of Oma, as I called her, in a white sleeveless dress and yellow terry towel hat holding an umbrella and standing by a sun-drenched field in Srebrnjak. She had come up to watch Štefek and Mila rake hay. The photo shows she didn't really fit into that world. That umbrella! But my father thought she did belong, in a sense. He said she belonged because she was willing to work however she could, like taking care of my little sister and me and helping in the kitchen with the cooking and afterwards with the dishes, which was an elaborate business, dumping the leftovers into the slop pail for the pigs, then using pails and plastic containers to wash up and then throwing the dirty water into the grass on the side of the house. I remember too how everyone told me that Oma was *dobra*, that she was a good woman. A part of this assessment was that she was willing to work, though she was under no obligation to work at all according to local customs when it came to guests.

With Oma there that summer, and other members of the Croatian family showing up, the kitchen became too crowded for our midday meal, so we ate outside. Many of these Sunday-type meals began with chicken or beef soup ladled out of big pots, the noodles in the soup having been prepared from fresh dough in the morning; this was followed by boiled meat with horseradish sauce, which I detested at the time; then a main course of roast pork or fried chicken pieces in a breaded coating, which I liked better, with pommes-frites or wide *mlinci* noodles fried in grease and bowls of sliced cabbage salad and green salad and plates piled with fat spring onions fresh from the garden and a basket of thick-hewn cornbread. Afterwards came cheese or apple strudel. The strudel appeared on big plates as if out of the blue, but I knew from my time later in Srebrnjak that Mila or Strina had grated the apples in the morning and rolled the dough flat on the kitchen table (the same table we were using outside), which was lightly dusted with flour. Then they had sprinkled oil on the dough and billowed it like a sheet in the wind before adding the grated apples and cheese and rolling up the dough in long sausages, ready to be put in the oven.

As I write, a memory comes back of my three-year-old sister refusing to eat any of the food in Srebrnjak, and my mother hitting upon the idea to mince some chicken liver and mix it with rice and lie to my sister that the result was "normal" Yugoslavian rice. I can still hear my father discounting my mother's worry, telling her, "Listen, if she gets hungry, she'll eat. Don't you worry. Quit your panicking!" Even then, though I didn't understand it at the time, my father's loud mockery and my mother's aversion to it, and her dismissing him with an annoyed click of her tongue, hinted already at my parents' different personalities and incompatibility.

After lunch, when the afternoon waned and there was less movement around the place, except Štefek with the wicker basket scything grass in the yard under the plum trees, I used to kick a soccer ball around. I played by myself, making moves and deking imaginary defenders. Strina Slava, sitting outside with my mother, giggled, covering her mouth with her hand to hide her teeth, and said, "Our Tony never walks anywhere!" My father, though he had coached our Parkview community league team to the Edmonton city championship three years before, was too busy talking politics and drinking wine to waste time playing with me in Srebrnjak. I can see him there now, glass in one hand, other hand gesticulating, probably explaining how great Canada was and how crappy Yugoslavia was. But as a boy he had played here too. In the late 1940s and early '50s, he and the other kids had made their ball out of pantyhose stuffed with newspaper and tied together with string so that the game only seemed to have begun before the ball disintegrated. If there wasn't enough food, there sure as hell wasn't any money to buy a real soccer ball!

I want to add here, before going any further, that everyone in Srebrnjak knew my father as "Joža," an informal version of "Josip" (Joseph). My mother, however, called him "Joe," as did all the kids on the Parkview Charlie Browns, and as I did too. I started to call him Joe because I had been influenced by some boyhood friends who lived across the alley from my grandparents—two brothers who addressed their artist professor parents from England by their first names, a habit that rubbed off on me for some reason. My father never corrected me. "Joe" he became and "Joe" he has always remained.

Near the end of our stay in 1977, Joe invited members of his family and their descendants to a pig roast. Among them was his half-brother, Ivek, one of the boys left behind with Strina Slava. Ivek never got to know either of his parents. His own mother died a few days after he was born, and his and Joe's father had died in the war. His second mother, Joe's birth mother, abandoned him for a man across the hill. And because there was no room in the little peasant house, he was forced to leave the only home he had known and move in with his grandfather in Rakitje. Yet he held things together. He got married, had kids, and lived a good life in Yugoslavia. Three years older than Joe, he had receding black hair, a fleshy nose, and a purplish complexion from drinking that his summer tan couldn't conceal. He took the time occasionally to talk to me, and when he spoke, he mumbled his words as though he'd just been at the dentist. Even when I got to know the language better, I had trouble understanding what he said. Mila, who had grown up with him, told me once that Ivek always had "stones in his mouth!"

Also at the pig roast was Joe's cousin from nearby Jagnić Dol, another Štefek Juranko. His character, however, was quite different from that of the Štefek Juranko who lived in Srebrnjak. He was a jovial man with laughter in his eyes and a round, dimpled Santa Claus nose who had a ready bag of jokes and stories in the company of others and poked fun at his wife and argued politics with his daughter. He kept rabbits in a hutch and owned a vineyard in the upper part of Srebrnjak. In his poorer years, back in the 1960s, he stretched out his pale wine so that he could sell it. It was Štefek from Jagnić Dol who left a mark forever on Joe's friend from Srebrnjak, Tonček Juranko, by slicing off the two middle fingers of his left hand with an axe when they were chopping wood as boys. "Don't worry, just hold the wood steady," Štefek had said. A cruel retribution came back to hurt Štefek in his later years when he was suffering from diabetes and had to have his toes amputated, then both feet, and eventually both legs. But to the end he was optimistic, Joe remembered, and clung to life.

At the pig roast, too, was one of Mila's two daughters, Marica, and her husband Miško, an amiable, shirt-off-the-back kind of guy whose principles and life lessons sometimes bordered on authoritarian dogma. Miško stood maybe 5'4", and even back in 1977 didn't have much hair, but did sport copious 1970s-style sideburns along the edges of his round head and had a gap between his front teeth. He taught driving in Samobor and drove a white Volkswagen beetle. He was a registered communist, though I didn't know this at the time, and kept a golden bas-relief of Tito on a wall in his house. He and his wife came to Srebrnjak every day, year after year, to help on the hill or in the garden. By contrast, Mila's other, younger, daughter and her husband arrived each Sunday for a meal, showing up with empty baskets and leaving with baskets filled with eggs, milk, cheese, and meat, as though they'd come to a grocery store. It was this younger daughter's husband who helped himself to a big apple I'd picked from the tree in the backyard and put in a wicker basket in the cellar as a present for Oma.

By the end of my Srebrnjak summer I was at home in the green fecund world of northern Croatia, with its rolling hills and head-high corn rustling in the wind, and with the plums that had already fallen to the ground stored in barrels for distillation. I'd become used to all the sounds of Srebrnjak also: the crowing of roosters first thing every morning and throughout the day; the sleepy clucking of hens and the cries of swallows that flew in and out of the barn; the pigs grunting and squealing when they were about to be fed; and the hooting of an owl somewhere distant (which wasn't an owl, it turned out, but a dove). All these sights and sounds of the summer in Srebrnjak became embedded in my mind. And so that is why my first trip to the alien landscape of the coast, especially to my first Croatian island, made such an impact on me as a kid.

FIGURE 4. Tony Fabijančić, with Srebrnjak in the background, 1977. Photograph by Ursula Fabijančić.

For the green boy of 1977, the island of Brač was exotic. Momentously, for me, it was the first island I ever visited, and vivid impressions stayed with me long afterwards—the fierce quality of the sun's light in the hot afternoons, the iridescent sea with its million black sea urchins, and the cobbled streets of old towns where donkeys dozed in the shade. It was a place like none I had seen before. My openness to adventure coincided perfectly with my arrival on an island, as though islands invited new experiences and greater adventures than the mainland, as if the ferry that sailed me across had taken me into a new world. And it was a new world, not only in the sense that I'd never seen it before, but because it was set apart from the land near it. As one Croatian writer put it, typically "you do not go to an island by road, you do not approach it on foot. You do not leave an island as you leave a village or a city. You suddenly put on shore, descending on an island like a seagull. You drop off an island just as the island itself dropped off from the shore and just as we disembark from a boat: only over a temporary, narrow and swaying bridge which is and yet is not a bridge."[2] So my feeling of adventure and discovery, which everyone knows is part of travelling anywhere, seemed concentrated into that first island experience. And the islands of Croatia in general called to me for years afterwards towards the end of every long winter or on those grey spring days when the mounds of snow got black and ugly, and when I longed to escape.

To get to Brač in 1977 we drove south from Zagreb along the Adriatic Sea in a white '72 Citroën, similar to the white '69 DS 21 Palas we still owned in Edmonton. There was no air conditioning, and the windows were shut because Oma was travelling with us and was worried she would catch a cold.

[2] Slobodan Novak, "Introspective Mirror," in *The Adriatic Archipelago Telling Tales*, translated by Stipe Grgas (Split: Hydrographic Institute of the Republic of Croatia, 2010), 129.

"Guck mal wie ich schwitze," she told us, wiping her forehead and showing us her wet hand. Then she would say, "Es zieht hier." "It's drafty here. If the windows are open, I could get sick."

"You're sweating because the windows are closed," Joe, answered. "If we opened them, it would be cooler."

"I'm a seventy-four-year-old woman, and I think I know what is best for me," she said. "I have been around a little longer than you. What would happen if I got sick? Do you want me to catch pneumonia?"

There was only one right response to this comment, and I think it was my mother who answered quickly. So, with every window shut except the driver's one, which Joe left open just an inch for a "little fresh air," we suffered penitently in the stifling heat the rest of the way. Naturally, it took us most of the day to arrive in the city of Split, from where ferries sailed to the islands, since we were forever slowing to a crawl behind convoys of trucks and campers and tourist buses on the Magistrala Highway that wound along precarious cliffs from Istria to Dubrovnik. Joe used to mock the Yugoslav communists for celebrating the highway as though it were one of the greatest engineering feats since the construction of the Great Wall of China. "And whaaat," he would say, drawing out his words as he did when he was mocking something, "and whaaaaat. A road that's no bigger than the one from Rakov Potok to Jastrebarsko, and that takes you all day to get from A to B. Big fucking deal!"

I don't remember much else about our road south except our stop at a Roma camp on the side of the highway, where a mangy brown bear was on show. In those days this was a common sight in Yugoslavia. The bear was muzzled, had a ring in its nose by which it was chained to a stake, and was forced by his master, a wizened old man with a leather face, baggy trousers and a whip in his belt, to get up on its hind legs and dance a few steps. Tourists could pay for a photo of themselves with the bear, but my mother didn't want to reward the man's mistreatment of the animal, and Joe didn't want to give the man any money, so no picture of that day exists.

After the bear, we made it to Split, Dalmatia's largest city, and from there we sailed to Brač. On deck, we were hit alternately by wafts of fresh sea air and cigarette smoke, a combination you can still count on in Dalmatia. We could see the blue-green island in front of us and behind us, the massive grey wall of the Mosor mountains on the mainland rearing over Split. In half an hour we were on the island. On a rough gravel road we ascended to a plateau. The land was dry, covered by olive groves and pine scrub and rock walls, and soon we descended the southern side of Brač, where we saw the Adriatic glitter in evening sunshine, and the long blue shadowy back of Hvar rising from the sea like a prehistoric beast.

Our stay in Brač wasn't notable for the resort in Bol, or our hotel, a rectangular communist structure typical of tourist spots in the former Yugoslavia with its big, framed photo of President Tito in the lobby, or our spartan, white-washed room. It was Bol's famous beach, Zlatni Rat (Golden Horn), a curving peninsula pointing into the green and blue water of the southern Adriatic that made our trip memorable. Anyone who sees it for the first time will agree it is a stunning beach. Yet, to my eyes, Zlatni Rat wasn't what it was cut out to be. It was crammed with tourists and there were cigarette butts and garbage everywhere. Plus, the sight of middle-aged German *Hausfrauen* greased heavily with suntan lotion, their breasts there for everyone to see, was an uncomfortable one for a sheltered kid from a chilly Canadian suburb of the 1970s.

To the boy in 1977 the beach was more beautiful in photographs, especially ones from the air, than it was on the ground. Later, I found this experience of disappointment confirmed in an essay by Walker Percy called "The Loss of the Creature." His main example is a contemporary sightseer's reaction on visiting the Grand Canyon for the first time. Unlike Garcia Lopez de Cardeñas, the first European to encounter the canyon, no one can experience all the awe of its visceral reality because it has been taken over by the "symbolic complex which has already been formed in the sightseer's mind."[3] All the photographs, travel pamphlets, as well as the name "Grand Canyon" itself, have established an image of the canyon long before the traveller ever actually reaches it.

In Walker Percy's example the pictures precede the reality, but I wonder if the reverse is possible too. In my case, not knowing anything about Zlatni Rat beforehand, I experienced the loss of the creature in Percy's sense *afterwards*, after seeing tourist brochures of Bol and thinking to myself that pictures of the beautiful empty beach taken from up high didn't really look like the thing itself. The beach seemed sandy from a distance, for example, when it was really made of stone shingles. Tourists, poor fools, were going to come all this way and be disappointed.

The upshot for Walker Percy when it comes to travelling is that an original experience is no longer possible, in the sense of an experience unfiltered and untouched by the symbolic complex. This would seem even truer since the arrival of the Internet, which floods us with information about a destination, exhausts its unique properties and lays bare its secrets. And it seems most true especially when it comes to famous places. But, as Percy himself goes on to write, you can try to recover the canyon by avoiding all the facilities for seeing the canyon, leaving the beaten path, approaching the canyon from a different angle, or you could try to see the object anew by deliberately searching for the most beaten track of all, a dialectical savouring of the familiar as the familiar. Or, more simply (and maybe this is what has guided me in the pages that follow), a traveller can take the position that even familiar, noisy and well-trodden locations reveal hidden images of themselves if you know how to look for them.

---

3 Walker Percy, *The Message in the Bottle* (New York: Picador, 1975), 47.

Here is an example of Percy's symbolic complex at work, the apocryphal story about Brač—the myth that the entire White House in Washington is made of Brač's white alabaster limestone or, to put it in the terms of local jingoism, that a relatively unknown island like Brač is important to a great country like America. Once you hear this story, you come to the island with a different attitude than you had before. And once you learn that the story is not true, your views change again. Even though some well-known structures around the world, including Diocletian's Palace in Split and Canada's Vimy Ridge Memorial in Flanders, are constructed from Brač's limestone, the White House is not. It is built out of Aquia Creek sandstone from Virginia, which is grey-brown and was only later painted white.[4]

Oma sat in the shade of the pines along Zlatni Rat while we roasted on the packed beach with thousands of loud, flaccid, partly nude Germans who had driven south in campers and were settled in equally congested RV parks. The water was beautifully turquoise at the edges where it met the land, but the beach was hot and painful on my winter-soft feet, and I concluded that overall Pigeon Lake near Edmonton, Alberta, where I was born, was just as nice. Had I gone a few hundred metres farther along the coast, as I did years later, I would have thought differently. There, in rocky inlets, the water taps out a gentle rhythm against the white pebbled shore, and from the pine trees the vigorous clacking of cicadas rises from the forest and floats out to sea like the whirring of summer popsicle sticks on the spokes of a thousand bicycles.

---

4 See Wendy Zentz, "Yugoslavs Claim Bit of White House," *South Florida Sun Sentinel*, 8 November 1986. According to Zentz, William Seale, author of *The President's House: A History* (Washington, DC: White House Historical Society, 1986), claims that alabaster limestone from Brač was used in the 1902 renovation of the White House.

A body experiences a different degree of pleasure lying on one of these small beaches than it does by a Prairie lake, probably one more akin to the experience in the South Pacific. The water is pleasant, almost too warm to be refreshing, but with the sun's heat against your skin and the aromas of the pine forest and the sea around you and the beat of cicadas, your body is almost perfectly in tune with the Dalmatian world. I remember another island that we visited a few years later, Maui, which was exotically fresh and distant from my normal world and my past self, an island whose sun and ocean all complemented my trip to Brač as though it and Brač belonged to the same chain of warm-water islands, and even though remote from each other in distance and geography, were linked naturally within my personal islands experience, becoming fused in my thoughts and dreams. It was my young age too, when I first touched down in the Pacific, that embedded a

FIGURE 5. Tony Fabijančić and Joe Fabijančić on the Adriatic coast, 1969. Photograph by Ursula Fabijančić.

certain attitude about the world into my island journeys to Croatia, most of which took place years later when I was older, much older. It injected all those later trips with the same joy of physical youth, the realistic (it seemed) impossibility of aging, decrepitude, and death that I knew at some other level would come soon enough. I was just sixteen, at that stage of my life when a curvy girl in an orange bikini caught my imagination and sent me off on fantastic daydreams, but when I still didn't have the guts to approach her. Joe egged me on futilely, "You'll be sorry one day, sonny boy, just you wait." I'd been landlocked in a new, sterile suburb where the trees hadn't grown yet. Maui, by contrast, was surrounded by the vast Pacific, and its great waves and beaches were warm, beautiful, and full of life. It gave me a sense of new possibilities. Anyone who has travelled here from a Canadian city in winter understands what I mean so I say nothing new, but for me arriving at Kahului airport became a memorable travel moment.

There's the opposite scenario—a traveller who comes from a benign climate, steps into the hostile wintry air of a northern region and experiences a shock to the body. This is what happened to Tonček Juranko, Joe's boyhood friend from Srebrnjak who flew into Edmonton on a freezing howler of a night in November 1970, still wearing the patent-leather shoes and sports jacket he'd become accustomed to in Rouen. Joe had tempted him to western Canada with talk of steak two inches thick and plentiful jobs that paid well (five bucks an hour!), but he knew he'd made a mistake the second he went outside. He said the icy air froze his throat and seized up his lungs and he couldn't breathe. He went right back to the ticket counter to ask about a return flight. Of course there was no return flight, not right away, so he was forced to stay a few days. When he arrived at Oma's house, she pulled him out of the cold and the snow and drew a bath for him. It was ironic, hilarious even, that the very person who had convinced him to leave France for Edmonton, Joe, was nowhere near the place that winter, but instead was enjoying the French Riviera in Palavas-les-Flots, not far to the south of Montpellier, where my mother was completing her doctorate. Tonček's temporary visit led to a few self-imposed, depressed weeks. He found he couldn't just up and leave for fear of being called a quitter and disappointing Joe, who was a big brother figure to him. His entry-level job as a machinist paid him just $2.50 an hour, not the five dollars he'd been promised, yet his stay stretched out impossibly to a few months, and then a few more months, and then a few years. Of course, he's been in Edmonton ever since . . .

While I spent my days on the beach in Maui, Oma, who was with us on another vacation, sat on a picnic bench under the palm trees. She smiled at me when I came up, sweeping her arm across the scene, "Oh wie herrlich, Tony! How glorious!" And yet, despite the beauty around us, her thoughts invariably returned to her native Schleswig-Holstein and to memories of her family. When she remarked how I enjoyed the water, she got to thinking about her older brother, Otto, who liked to swim too. Pictures of the thatched roofs of Großenbrode and the sand dunes of the cool Baltic coast swept over her and she was back in 1912 with her brother. Otto had no fear of the water, and swam in all conditions, even where he wasn't supposed to, like under the gate in the harbour and out to sea. The little girl watched him go, a pale phosphorescent flash in a blue-grey sea, watched him as he struck out with confident strokes. He was a real athlete, and a good boy, such a good boy, Oma told me, with blond hair and blue eyes, a typical northern German.

I have a black-and-white photo of Otto in uniform wearing his sailor's cap, with the name of his division on the band. He was eighteen. Now when I look at him, I don't see myself, but my son, who is just as blond as Otto, and who could have been his younger brother. Like Otto, he too likes to take physical risks, and isn't afraid of the ocean. And when I see him dive off some rocks on a beach in Nova Scotia and descend to the

bottom, then resurface bran-
dishing a lobster, I think a bit
of Otto must be inside of him.

Of course, these thoughts
could not have come to me as
I sat with Oma on the bench
above the beach under the
palm trees. I was bored of her
stories because I'd heard many
of them before, but I was loyal
to them also because I knew
she was old and her health
wasn't good. She had suffered
an aneurysm five months before and had nearly died. Her

FIGURE 6. Otto Bartschek, ca.
1918. Photographer unknown.

hair hadn't quite grown back fully where it had been shaved.
And even though she always brought a book with her to the
beach—*Buddenbrooks*, by Thomas Mann—she never managed
to get beyond the first page. The past, though, always seemed
to come back easily to her.

As we sat on her bench, she told me the rest of Otto's story.
An irony of his life was that the boy who could swim so well
died at sea. During the Battle of Jutland, around three in the
morning on 1 June 1916, the SMS *Pommern* was torpedoed by
the British destroyer *Onslaught*. Otto and 838 other crewmen
went down in the dark with the ship. The loss for Oma was
still fresh, and it crossed the decades and arrived here, on a
glorious day, as the blue waves rolled in and the sounds of
children playing reached her on her bench.

"Ach, Tony, meine Mutter, meine arme Mutter sie wollte
sterben." Her mother, she said, had wanted to die.

After telling me the story, Oma was quiet for a while, then
went back for lunch, and I took a last swim. With new, special vigour I threw myself against the waves and dove to the
bottom where the sun on the corrugated surface cast flickering

shadows and I rode one wave after another, imagining as I did so that I was swimming under the gate and out to sea, like Otto, with confident strokes. In those moments the afternoon sun shone harder and with more heat than before, and the blue of Maalaea Bay was bluer than ever. Later, when I was tired, I sat on the bench above the beach and, in the place where Oma had been before, I took a last look around. I tried to memorize the scene, the blue sea, the clouds, to remember all the little things—my habit when I was leaving a place for good. I stayed for a while, then I picked up my towel and started back.

So, in that moment, Maallaea Bay was for me what the Adriatic Sea would always be, a place that made me feel good to be alive. The hedonistic attraction of the coast was obvious, but even the Croatian islands' tough arid country on summer afternoons when the candent sun beats every living thing into submission, and when the wooden doors and windows in towns and villages are shut tight, gave me the same feeling of the marrow of life. More than once I wandered out in midday, sometimes under the pressures of my writing, at other times for no other reason than the craziness of youth. Each of these walks was different yet the same: a country road alongside a vineyard or a meadow of lavender or a garden; swallows skimming over the ground, carving the warm blue air; olive trees, stooped and gnarled, cantankerous, their dusty leaves quivering, silver underneath; corridors of black pines along a sea walk carpeted by brown needles, the lean of the trees telling the direction of the prevailing wind, and white clouds schooning on the horizon, heading out to sea. And always, the Adriatic in its usual daytime summer mood, green near shore and deeper blue farther out, perhaps torn with patches of white if the wind was up, but always pleasantly cooling on my body, on my sun-blasted head.

Learning to Fly

It would be ten years before I returned to Yugoslavia. My parents gifted me a trip there after I'd graduated from St. Francis Xavier University in Antigonish, Nova Scotia with a degree in English. I went on my own because we couldn't all of us afford to travel. We'd moved to Antigonish a few years before when my mother landed a tenure-track position in the Department of Modern Languages, and because Joe wanted to get the hell out of Edmonton finally. He had never liked its freezing winters or mosquito summers and thought anywhere else would be better, and his real estate business in Edmonton was failing because of the recession in the early 1980s. Little did he know that the cliquishness of small-town Nova Scotia was going to kill his job prospects. (He once applied for a job as a janitor with a local construction company and was told by the boss that he was "overqualified"!) For years, Joe didn't have work in Antigonish other than cooking and cleaning, taking over the role of housewife, which wasn't what he had envisioned for himself when he left Edmonton. Later, he worked at a machine shop in Dartmouth (he was a machine fitter by trade), putting in long hours of overtime and sleeping all week in the back of our Chrysler LeBaron station wagon to save money. It was this last decision some people in Antigonish remember well. The editor of *The Antigonish Review* at the time, George Sanderson, recalled Joe decades later, and told me once when I was at his office about a story I had submitted (it was the same day he handed me a copy of Walker Percy's essay on the loss of the creature), that what Joe did was quite something. There is a lot to unpack there. The irony was that the more Joe thought he was doing, the more it was all slipping away. But that is another story.

The LeBaron station wagon, by the way, was the same vehicle he and I drove out west in in 1988, me to carry on with my M.A. at the University of Victoria in British Columbia, he to help me along and to find work at another machine shop. We too slept in the car every night on our trip across the USA. Somewhere on a long straight stretch in South Dakota, my foot got heavy on the pedal and the LeBaron hit ninety miles an hour. A highway cop coming the other direction flashed his lights at us, turned around and ticketed us $100. "You can pay me now, or you can wait for the judge in town," he told us. "Your choice. But the judge is on holidays and ain't gonna be back 'til next week. Maybe." Joe was pissed. Nevertheless, he handed the man a hundred-dollar bill. There went the money we'd saved sleeping in the car. We spent the next night in a motel.

Travelling to Yugoslavia by myself for the first time after having graduated that spring gave me a sense of freedom, release, and nervous anticipation. I was tired after my red-eye flight but alert and excited at seeing the villages again. More of the houses were façaded with white plaster this time; that was a difference I noticed, but everything else looked the same. Iron gates around each yard, plum and apple orchards, sunburnt peasants on tractors pulling loads of hay. I saw hundreds of Yugoslav soldiers digging a ditch beside the road for telephone wires. At the turnoff for Srebrnjak the weathered, wooden crucifix at the entrance to the valley was still there, and the road was still gravel. When we got to the house, I saw it was covered by white plaster now. For a moment, I was astonished that the house had been here the entire time I was gone, that the people had been going through each day, working each day as they always had, without me to witness them and bring them to life.

My second cousin, Vlado, had picked me up at the airport. A medical student at the University of Zagreb, he asked me if I wanted to stay at his parents' place in the nearby village of Jagnić Dol rather than being stuck out there in Srebrnjak—that was basically how he put it, but out of loyalty to my father and the people there and my memories of my past visit I guess (I was even then a creature of habit), I declined his offer.

When we arrived, it was a late Saturday afternoon. Members of the family were sitting around the kitchen table. Strina Slava was on her wooden box, and when she stood up to greet me, kissing me on both cheeks, she seemed small and frail. Mila had gained weight, wore glasses, and didn't pinch me on the cheek as she had before. Štefek, since I'd had little contact with him the last time, and had only a hazy memory of him, was a figure that was newer and more unfamiliar than the women, yet with his cap, worker's clothes and strong peasants' hands, seemed like an archetype as much as a person I didn't remember well. The two daughters were there with their husbands—the friendly round-headed driving instructor, Miško, and the other one, a less friendly but confident and charismatic loudmouth.

I didn't know much of the language then, so Vlado translated their questions and my answers. He said, "You should be free to say how you feel. We are honest people, and we say what we think." For a while I thought there was some irony about his remark about freedom of expression in a country that wasn't a paragon of free thought, since he was a stalwart Yugoslav, not a nationalist Croat. Joe told me, for example, that after World War Two Štefek's younger brother was nearly hanged for remarks he allegedly made against the Partisans. But obviously things weren't so sensitive now, and Vlado probably meant regular thoughts and feelings, not political ones. Joe said, however, that there was never any worry in that house about saying the wrong thing or being "reported" by someone.

The sun was shining through the windows in the white-walled kitchen, which had a white wood stove, a table and chairs and a black-and-white TV in the corner. I felt happy to be there, and even though I didn't understand much unless Vlado translated, I felt I belonged. A little over-confidently at one point, I asked the loudmouth son-in-law a question for some reason. He was the one who ten years before had eaten the apple I'd picked as a gift for Oma when she was to arrive in Srebrnjak, and that I'd placed on top of a basket of apples in the cellar rather proudly. He had eaten it without knowing its importance to me, but I never forgave him. I asked him if he felt happy, and his taciturn response and dismissive shrug were probably justified, "That's not something I need to answer." I wonder whether this question of mine, when he and his wife, Mila's younger daughter, were going to the coast with their son later that summer, came back to bite me, made him decide he didn't have room for me *and* the TV set in their car. As a result, I didn't make it to the coast that year.

On this same afternoon when I arrived, I noticed some changes to the house. Upstairs was a new bathroom with a toilet and tub. Joe had given Štefek money and he'd finally gone ahead with the construction. I was pleasantly surprised. I remember being worried before I left on this trip about where I was going to wash, and Joe had said, "You'll just go outside in the back with a pail, and just tell them not to look at you! *Nemoj gledati!* It will be warm so don't worry, sonny boy. It's hot in the summer!" He had a laugh at my expense.

The shower in the tub was connected to a tall water heater with a stove at the bottom. They used dried corncobs for fuel, and every Saturday Mila would start a fire in the late afternoon for her and Štefek's weekly bath together. Even though there was no closeness between the two of them during the day, not that I ever saw, here was some breaking of bread or whatever each Saturday. Either that or it was more economical to kill two birds with one stone, or to put it differently, wash two bodies with one bucket of corncobs.

Much of my Yugoslavia experience in 1987 was in Srebrnjak and followed a similar pattern. Each morning Mila cooked me a breakfast of fried eggs and cornbread, or žganci, which was corn or wheat meal in chunks slathered with pork grease. Štefek had a bowl of žganci pieces floating in coffee diluted with milk and, like my father, ate with similar concentration and speed. Mila also made me *majčina dušica* tea ("mother's soul") from some flowers that grew in the valley. Often I had a shot of *šljivovica* after breakfast, a morning custom among men there at that time, and sat outside the front door, buzzed a bit, because I was new to hard liquor, listening to the sounds of the day like the hooting of a dove somewhere and the occasional crow of a rooster, plus the noises from the kitchen as Mila prepared lunch, added wood to the stove, and so on. Smells wafted out through the open window in the late morning: a simmering pot of cabbage, beef or chicken soup, the cornbread cooling on a board on the windowsill or, on some days, meat roasting in the oven.

Now and again I would go inside to chat with Mila and see how lunch was progressing, or I would chug back a glass of water I'd put in the fridge, which caused her to warn me not to drink water so cold, one of the many examples of peasant lore about the body I heard while in Srebrnjak (another was that I should never sit on the ground, even in the summer, because doing so could make me sick). Or I would talk to her through the open window and let her know that Vlado the mailman was coming on his motorbike, or a woman was approaching selling clothing in a wicker basket or a Roma on a horse-drawn wagon looking for scraps of metal. Mila would step outside and yell out, "We don't have anything." Around one o'clock she would leave the kitchen, stride out into the yard, and holler up the hill, "Štefek, *odi jest*," then return and tell me, "Come and eat, Tony." Then we would begin without him. Whatever it was we were eating, she would say much the same thing year after year: "Tony, *uzmi*—take" and I would help myself, and then she would say, "Take some more" or "Why don't you take some more?" or "*Samo ječ*—Just eat." If I complimented her on the food, invariably she would tell me to take more, *uzmi još*, and then I would reply, "No, thanks," and she would laugh and say, "Then it mustn't have been that good." And I would retort, "How much am I supposed to eat?" Soon after we started eating, Štefek arrived from the hill and told me "*Dobar tek*—bon appétit," hung his hat on a hook and washed his hands and then went to the shaving mirror by the front window, combed back the thin strands of his hair and gave himself a final once-over. Then he was ready to eat.

Another part of my day that summer was reading every morning outside the kitchen. I had recently discovered Henry Miller, whose brash, Rabelaisian vulgarity and anti-establishment views were consistent with my own rebellious ideas, which were bookish and never put to practice. The buzz from the šljivovica, a full stomach, the new freedom from my family, the adventure of being in a country that was still new to me, all aligned perfectly with the writing of Henry Miller. I had a paperback of *Black Spring* with me that summer, and even though it concentrated mostly on Brooklyn, Manhattan, and Paris at the start of the twentieth century, its wildness and effusiveness arrived in my life at the right time. This passage from "A Saturday Afternoon" is typical of the book: "At the St. Cloud bridge I come to a full stop. I am in no hurry—I have the whole day to piss away. I put my bicycle in the rack under the tree and go to the urinal to take a leak. It is all gravy, even the urinal. As I stand there looking up at the house fronts a demure young woman leans out a window to watch me. How many times have I stood thus in this smiling, gracious world, the sun splashing over me and the birds twittering crazily, and found a woman looking down at me from an open window, her smile crumbling into soft little bits which the birds gather in their beaks and deposit sometimes at the base of a urinal where the water gurgles melodiously."[5]

I did some writing myself too, upstairs in the attic, because it was quiet and had a small table and chair by the dried corn-cobs piled up to the rafters in one corner, even though the attic became as hot as a sauna by mid-morning.

I didn't feel any negativity about this intellectual activity of mine from anyone living in that house, and never from the oldest and least educated people there. Instead it was Miško, the driving instructor son-in-law, who remarked, "Reading again?" or "This writing of yours better lead to something" or "What does all this thinking do for you, for your brain? You're going to hurt yourself with too much thinking." In retrospect I suspect he was just ribbing me good-naturedly, but at the time I was pissed off at him. He wasn't my father, was he? but there he was making comments. I lacked the self-confidence of Henry Miller, and Miško's remarks produced self-doubt in me. I started to stick to my room whenever I wrote or cracked open a book. If I, with all that support for reading growing up, could become self-conscious about it, I wondered how others like me would have fared in this world. How many others were there who had been stifled by the pressure? My mother told me that at some point she had tried to teach Strina Slava the Croatian alphabet after Strina had expressed, with a sigh, the wish to be able to read. Her schooling with my mother didn't last very long because everyone there made fun of her, and she became too shy to continue.

5 Henry Miller, *Black Spring* (New York: Grove Press, Inc., 1963), 37.

Another thing I did with regularity that summer was go running; that is, running *for exercise*. I ran all around the area, especially along the crest of the Srebrnjak hill to the Marija Magdalena chapel. Mila said that someone in Mala Gorica who had seen me running had called me a *luđak*, a lunatic. Mila's laughter at my expense reminded me of Joe's when he mocked me about something. The story had travelled from Mala Gorica and across the hill to Srebrnjak and to Mila's ears. She hadn't left her yard, she rarely left her yard except maybe to get her hair permed at the salon in Sveta Nedelja, yet somehow she had heard this bit of gossip as though it had arrived on the wind or had been transported by some mysterious peasant telepathy. The person in Mala Gorica had thought I was crazy because there was no understanding or acceptance among peasants of an activity like running; they thought it was for people with too much time on their hands, too much *leisure* time, people who didn't have serious work to do. Plus, what sort of fool runs in the heat when he doesn't have to?

That summer, as I had before, I followed Strina Slava around the yard while she did her chores. Even though Mila had taken over the heavy work, Strina still contributed. Work never stopped for people here. They worked until they dropped, and when they couldn't work anymore their family put them on the wood box or on a couch in the kitchen or in the bed upstairs. But Strina was still active and useful. She and I talked a fair amount; I was learning more of the language each day. She chattered on about simple things, talked to the animals she was feeding, told me what she had to do next. She smiled and called me *lijepi dečko*, handsome boy. I watched her pluck nettles with her bare hands and take them to the barn and chop them with a hatchet. The chopping block was on a table and had a dip in it from all the chopping. She mixed the results with corn grain, went outside, and called, "Puro, puro, puro," and the turkeys gathered. She watched them eat, laughed at them for their behaviour, and swore at them for their stupidity.

Strina Slava wasn't treated well by her daughter. I don't think Mila ever addressed her except to criticize or mock her. For a long time, I thought Mila had inherited this hostility from Štefek, who never looked at Strina or even acknowledged she existed. I don't think I ever heard them talk to each other. I'd arrived at the conclusion that he thought of her as a third wheel who was more irritating than useful. One time, while Strina was plucking a slaughtered chicken in hot water, she said, a little simply and childishly, "What a beautiful chicken," admiring its plumpness, I guess. Mila shot back, "Beautiful chicken?! Shut up! It's a chicken, that's all it is. Just a damn chicken!" But on other occasions, Strina showed some backbone and ripped off a retort that shut Mila up. "You are wrong to think she was all soft," Joe told me. "She hated strife, but if she was pushed too far, don't worry, she could respond." Mostly her days were spent by herself, either working or resting on her box by the stove. At night, she rubbed šljivovica on her arthritic knees. Every month or so, she spent the night at her daughter's, over the hill in Dol. This was the house in which Jana lived, Mila's sister and Vlado's mother. I can remember Strina there in the summer kitchen, the one separate from the house, cheerfully sitting on a stool or peeling potatoes as Jana cooked or went around the yard doing other chores, and Strina Zora strode in, a strong-legged local gossip with a staved-in toothless face who spoke loudly and turned her head with the sharp nervous movements of a chicken. Mainly women filled the outdoor kitchen with their talk, gossip, and cheerfulness. I think that must have been Strina's reason for visiting; the mood back home was unfriendly and unpleasant, but here she felt relaxed and comfortable.

I didn't give much thought to Strina's situation at the time. Like most young guys, I concentrated mainly on myself. I was just enjoying the summer. I had started to loosen up as I hadn't so far in my life, didn't hesitate to talk at a full table of family and friends in my Croatian patois, newly improved by Vlado who came home tired from university but still found time to teach me. I wasn't afraid to crack a joke or tell a simple story, to set the table on a roar, discovering an ability I didn't know I had, everyone favourably disposed to me because I wasn't silent and inhibited. That summer was a turning point in my life given the uncertain, diffident, and even aloof person I'd been in my undergrad years, though the cliquishness of little Antigonish for sure had a role to play in that. Now in this environment with this extended "Yugoslav" family backing me, or at least focussing on me for a few months, I began to change and grow.

Drink in the
Summer

Between 1988 and 1990 I returned to Croatia three more times, when it was still part of Yugoslavia. No one knew the hell that was to come, and life in those summers with its peaceful and predictable normality seemed destined to go on forever. The end of Yugoslavia turned out to be the political and military counterpoint to the gradual coming-to-an-end of peasant life in the region where I always went. But that hadn't happened yet.

Across the hill in Dol I met a man Štefek's age, born in 1924 or so, but different from him in every way. While Štefek had joined Tito's communist Partisans and my grandfather the nationalist Domobrani, Slavko Jakopač had originally fought with the Germans, who were allied with the Croatian Ustaše, the fascists who ran the Axis-occupied part of the country from 1941 to 1945. His hatred for the Partisans and communists never waned, although at a critical moment during the war, when he saw the tide turning, he'd abandoned his German-run unit and joined the Partisans, a decisive and shrewd move that probably saved his life. Now he liked to hurl brickbats at the communists every chance he got. I remember him pulling out a few dinars from his wallet, tossing them to the ground and stomping on them. "This is communist money, *scheisse!*" Knowing my background, he sometimes spoke German to me, what pigeon he dimly recalled from the war. He was a big man with a big, cropped head and meaty hands who moved them around when he talked. "Dies ist junge Mann!—This is a young man," he yelled at me, "Aber dies ist alt, scheiss alt!— This one's old, old as shit," pointing at himself.

He was in the yard that belonged to Mila's sister, Jana, and her husband Dragec, because he owned a tractor, a John Deere he pronounced "John Deery," and had been paid to pick up hay from one of their parcels of land. That's how he earned extra money. I don't know whether he was commenting on his earnings that afternoon. Probably there was a going rate, and he was happy to get it. Jana listened to him as she always did, with some skepticism and probably distaste, because she was a civil woman who didn't approve of his loud, vulgar swagger.

I, on the other hand, having just discovered Henry Miller, liked Slavko and enjoyed talking to him, enjoyed his mouthy wildness as though Miller had somehow been reincarnated in the body of this Croatian nationalist stranded in this socialist country, even though they were very different politically. No one I met in Yugoslavia spoke out against the Yugoslav government or the system as much as Slavko did. Mind you, I didn't have political conversations with people I knew either. Conversations of the sort I had with Slavko had probably happened among people there long before I showed up, and everyone knew where everyone stood. Maybe they didn't trust me, or maybe they had no criticisms. Probably it was the latter. After all, life in this part of Yugoslavia was humming along reasonably well on its tracks towards the distant goal of a workers' paradise that people all probably knew was either far off given the present social and economic conditions, or total crap. And people in this region at least had the security of jobs in factories, state-owned stores, and so on, plus their own land. They were forced to work hard but weren't starving either.

I used to sit at a table outside Slavko's house drinking *gemišt* on hot mornings, listening to him blast the communists or relive his war years or just joke around. During the war he'd found himself in some precarious situations, the most dangerous of which was in the middle of the war when he and members of his unit had been lined up by the Partisans to be executed, but a firefight had ensued like a godsend. When the bullets spared him, he'd thrown himself down among the others and had gone still. Somehow in the chaos he just waited it out, then crawled out from the pile of bodies, his hands still wired together, and left his unit and made his way back home, back to this valley, where his family saw a gaunt, bearded ragged young man at their door.

At the end of the war, he witnessed hangings of convicted political "criminals" from the Russian poplars on the straight road between Sveta Nedelja and Samobor, the road of concrete slabs built by the Germans that survived until 2013, solid as hell. He saw the Partisans stand these men on stools and noose their necks. "Then kick the stool. Down. Bam. Dead!" he yelled, knocking my arm with the back of his hand and kicking the leg of the table to demonstrate, jolting the wine out of our glasses. "That was communism. That was Tito."

"Shit," I said.

"For them, yes," Slavko shouted back. "But what the hell, what do we care now, here we are! Drink, young man. Drink in the summer!"

He poured more wine into our glasses, and I added water, and he knocked his glass against mine, the wine spilling onto the table. "*Živjeli!*" he yelled.

Slavko lived alone in the big, cavernous four-bedroom brick house. His wife had died three or four years ago, and what remained of her memory inside was a small crucifix on a wall in the kitchen. His two sons no longer lived with him.

The older of the two drove a transport truck to Germany and would soon be arrested and imprisoned for running contraband, while the other was a louche, handsome guy nicknamed *Lepica* (The Moth), for his late nights out at bars, who was shot dead in the chest at a drunken card party at the start of the war in 1991.

Jana and Dragec owned land in Bušićka, one valley south of Srebrnjak, so more than once I helped them load a wagon of hay. The occasion about which I am writing was a rowen sometime in August. Dragec had scythed the hill the evening before, leaving the drying and transportation of hay to his wife who didn't hold a job outside the one at home and had time during the day for such chores.

Slavko drove Jana on John Deery. I rode by bicycle with Vlado's sister, Željka. An engineering student at the University of Zagreb, she was younger and prettier than her brother, with a mole on the bridge of her nose and straight jet-black hair down to her shoulders which, when she had menial chores to do, she wore in a ponytail, showing her pale neck. Her paleness distinguished her from her mother, whose brown summer skin told you where she spent most of her time. Jana always hoped her daughter was destined for something greater than a life on the land, supporting and accepting her long hours of study, and yet Jana often bickered with Željka about her lack of enthusiasm for farm work, especially during the summer when lectures had ended and the excuse of some distant exam on the horizon rang a little hollow. I can no longer remember exactly what drew me to Željka at first other than her prettiness, but she entered my life at the right time, the first girl I'd spent any extended time with, spoke to at any length, even though she was my second cousin.

We arrived in Bušićka and got to work while Slavko sat on the tractor smoking a cigarette. With pitchforks we turned over the bands of cut grass. It was noon. After ten minutes,

Jana said to me, "Tony, it is hot, you should rest. Go to the shade and rest." To Željka she said, "You missed that spot over there. Can't you do it properly?" To show Jana the work wasn't hard work for a fit young guy like me, I bounded around with my pitchfork, turning over the grass with energy, jumping over the rows of hay, sometimes in my haste jamming the steel into the ground. What a fool!

Within half an hour we were done. Slavko tossed his cigarette to the ground and we drove back to Dol.

After lunch, Slavko returned to Jana's house, this time towing a wooden leiter-wagon. Jana sat on a board behind Slavko, facing backwards. Željka and I sat on the wagon, our legs dangling over the edge. On the gravel road into Bušićka we bounced around on the boards. "Hey, this is fun," I yelled to Željka. We always spoke English and she answered, "Maybe it is fun once or two times but imagine doing this work all your life, all of it, year after year. I don't think this wagon would feel so fun then!"

The grass had dried since we'd turned it at noon. We set to work piling hay ricks with our pitchforks, pushing hay down from the top of the hill, then collecting the grass with wooden-toothed rakes. This time Slavko got off his tractor and helped toss big grass mounds onto the wagon. The work was harder than before, especially when the pile on the wagon got high. The late afternoon sun, poised now above the crest of the western hill, blazed on us. We were sweating; Željka's pale face was flushed and sweat dribbled down her cheeks and neck. I wanted to take off my shirt, but I remembered Štefek warning me not to do that because bits of grass could collect on your sweating body as well as flies and, even worse, ticks.

After working for a while, we took a break. From a bag, Jana brought out a wicker demi-john of white wine, a bottle of mineral water, and glasses. Slavko started to chafe Jana, which he did, I suppose, because he suspected she didn't approve of him or had some negative attitude towards him that he was never going to shed. "Hey Tony, look at this woman, look at her work. It's something to have a woman like that, a very good woman, very moral, better than the rest of us, and look at those strong legs!" He laughed and I laughed a little, and Jana smiled ruefully, shook a roguish finger at him and said, maybe a little stiffly because she didn't have experience countering this sort of wise-guy talk, the casual banter of men, "You just make sure you get this load back home in one piece."

Like her mother, Željka didn't share my enthusiasm for Slavko. She thought his talk and bluster concealed something else. "I don't know what it is, but he is hiding something. Maybe from the war. He seems happy on the outside, but I don't think he is. I think he is very unhappy, maybe in despair."

We were finished in Bušićka. Slavko and I hoisted a log timber on top of the hay pile and roped it down to keep everything in place on the drive back to Dol. Željka and I clambered on top of the hay and sat there on high, back-to-back, ducking when we passed under low-hanging branches, and laughing when the branches strafed us. Our ride on the fragrant hay was more pleasant and more cushioned than it was on the way here and the view grander from above. My satisfaction at having finished a job, plus the wine I had drunk, and finding myself on top of a wagon of hay where I could see far and people could see me and I was sitting with a girl for the first time with her body pressed against mine, a situation that was new to me, all of it had put me in a good mood.

Back in the yard Slavko reversed the wagon into the barn, unhitched it and went home. The job of hoisting the hay into the loft was waiting for Dragec and a next door neighbour, a mountain of a man called Milivoj, the son of the gossip Strina Zora. He and Dragec, in expert metronomic pas-de-deux, flung the hay up top while Jana distributed the hay in the loft, and then when they were done, they strewed a couple boxes of salt in the grass.

Afterwards, we sat at the table outside the kitchen, ate and drank gemišt. Milivoj was a huge guy with massive hands, but a boyish face flushed at the cheeks from working and a dense wiry head of curly brown hair. Shirtless, he sat across from me and spoke very simply so I could understand him, and I answered similarly, so that we must have come across as a couple of idiots. "Tony," he said, "you work very much today. You good man. Strong man. Show me hand." I showed him my blistered hands, which made him laugh good-naturedly, "Not worry, you work more, you strong! Here, živjeli!" I said to him, "Maybe I strong, okay, but not as strong as you, strong like Milivoj. Milivoj is big boy! *Veliki dečec!*" The last word I used, *dečec*, is a diminutive for "boy," and in effect meant "little boy," so I was calling giant Milivoj a big little boy. That made him smile, and Dragec laugh outright, and probably repeat to us ten times over the next few summers because Dragec was a recidivist when it came to telling jokes and bon mots, going back to the well a few times for the same laugh.

Dragec was a tall man, though not Milivoj's height, with intelligent bright eyes and wiry grey, cropped hair that stuck up from his head like the quills of a hedgehog. Typically, he wore slacks and a collared short-sleeved shirt tucked in and crisply ironed. That was Jana's doing. Now after working he wore only an undershirt. A teacher long ago had convinced his father, when his father had wanted Dragec to quit school, to let the boy continue, with the understanding that he be let out early every day to help on the land. So that was a cachet Dragec privately carried with himself throughout life while he worked as a labourer at the cement company *Samoborka*, and it helped instill, with Jana, who had also been forced to leave school early, the importance of education in his two kids.

On the question of education the husband and wife agreed but on other things they didn't see eye to eye, especially when it came to work, who was doing what, who was working harder, who could make the other feel guilty for not doing this or that fast enough, in the right order, and so on. But on a night like this when work was done, when the pressure was off for a while, everything ran smoothly. Dragec sat there with his gemišt, tossing out a few last queries about jobs that had to be done, and she answered "*Je sam*" or something else to the affirmative, and he responded with "*Dobro!*—Gooood," stretching out the word and adding a lilt to it to show his relaxed satisfaction and okayness with everything.

There we all sat; even Jana eventually came to eat, and Slavko showed up to tow his trailer back home, but not before a gemišt and more conversation. When darkness began to settle on the yard everyone dispersed. I sat with Željka on the steps for a while talking, watching the swallows fly in and out of the barn and then the bats begin to circle the streetlights, and the fireflies in the grass by the garden.

In Srebrnjak life was going on as it had before. Štefek was entering his seventies lean and fit and otherwise unchanged. Strina was more stooped and slow-moving and had a growth of some kind on her nose that she tried to scratch off every night with her fingernails, leaving a bloody scab. Mila, despite her cheerfulness around me, lumbered through the yard with familiar heaviness. She had begun to shoulder even more of the workload because her mother wasn't up to it any longer.

Mila and I chatted every day. I continued to sit outside the kitchen in the mornings and throw my two cents back through the open window and Mila would answer. Often, I scouted the traffic on the road, which was very slow in those days, every vehicle a sort of special event that drew Mila to the door to check out. I informed her when the Avon lady had stopped at the neighbours, which was an exciting moment for Mila because she could buy a cream to salve her cracked hands. One day, when Mile, a Croatian Jew who worked in Frankfurt, drove past I asked, "Where is Mile going?"

"What do I know?" Mila said. "Maybe back to Frankfurt."

"He's building a house here. It's not finished yet, so he's sleeping in the barn."

"If he would work faster, he could get out of the barn."

"He likes going slow. He says he's not in a rush. He's going to put the washroom in next year."

"He's a fool," Mila said.

"He says he likes the process."

"If you're building a house," Mila said, "then build your house."

I had no answer to that logic.

When my stay was coming to an end, I floated the idea of sleeping on a bench in the Frankfurt airport before my flight home the next day to save money on a hotel. Not hesitating, she said to me, "*Spavaj kao čovjek*—Sleep like a human. Sleep in a hotel."

As I said, life in Srebrnjak was going on as it had before. However, the collective work with neighbours and the camaraderie I'd experienced over in Dol, which was common in the former Yugoslavia, was absent at Štefek and Mila's.

FIGURE 7. Štefek and Mila outside their front door, ca. 1996

True, their older daughter Marica and son-in-law Miško helped daily but no one else from the village did, not even Štefek's brother, Marko, who lived in the ochre-façaded house next door. Never in all the years I spent in Srebrnjak do I remember Marko helping his brother, or vice versa. At the time I thought this had to do with some old grievance because Štefek had decided to marry Mila against his father's wishes and had moved into her family's house across the road, a decision that insulted and embarrassed his old man. The two apparently didn't speak for twenty years. And when he needed some help, the old man got a third party to ask his son over. They would work for hours, side by side, without talking. In any case, Štefek had disenthralled himself from the rest of the village, was proud and self-sufficient.

The house in Srebrnjak wasn't completely without society. People wandered in from all over, mostly needing something or buying something. I saw bowlegged, hard-bitten Pavek Lacković saunter in from his village carrying a bottle he wanted filled with šljivovica. A confrere of hard drinkers, it seemed he'd run out up there in the village of Lacković Breg at the very top of Srebrnjak. I'd been to Lacković Breg before, a more primitive village than Srebrnjak, with smaller cramped brick houses and muddy shit-covered yards and wild slathering dogs that pulled hard on their chains when strangers passed. Lacković Breg was what villages around here probably looked like in 1950. Štefek took the bottle, gave it a once-over because it had a cloudy look, and went into the cellar. Lacković stood just inside the threshold, waiting, rocking back and forth on his bandy legs, either uninterested in sitting down at the kitchen table or not invited to do so. Štefek handed him the full bottle and accepted the money politely— it couldn't have been more than seven or eight bucks in our present money—and gave it to Mila, who put it in an envelope in a kitchen cabinet. They said a few parting words and then he followed Lacković out the door and went on with his work.

There were other visitors. People from neighbouring villages came for water in the summer because their well had dried up, and this well was known to run deep no matter what. Štefek didn't like handouts but he sure wasn't averse to being generous himself. He never demanded a single dinar. "I always have water, so why shouldn't I help someone who needs it?"

Other visitors included white-collar residents of Zagreb who owned weekend houses in the upper part of the valley. One woman, whose name escapes me, showed up from time to time in her dresses and heels to pick up a new supply of Mila's hard ripened cheese and sour cream. The contrast between this stout middle-aged city lady and the peasants who lived there, as she stood in the little kitchen stiffly on her block heels emitting some kind of Yugo perfume, affecting sophistication, was funny to me. But she annoyed me too because she eventually turned my way and asked me who I was and what I was doing there as though she were checking out my credentials and right to be in the house, assuming the authority to ask, then wondered whether I was going to the coast, a typical question to visitors, as I struggled to communicate adequately at her level of Croatian. So, she had that over me. Another time, I got annoyed by the woman because she ignored me completely and conversed only with Štefek and Mila as though I weren't even in the room, which made me feel slighted by her—who did she think she was anyway?! Mila spoke to this person as she spoke to everyone, there was no change, but Štefek wasn't the same man. His sometimes-stilted manner of talking and his stiff hand gestures were exaggerated in the presence of the lady from Zagreb as though his moment on stage tightened him up badly and, like Polonius in the presence of the king and queen, he became ingratiating, a little sycophantic. Or maybe that wasn't what it was at all. Maybe I've just misread him. When she left, he went right back to work, striding a little faster, as though he had to catch up with his other self who hadn't been delayed by the city lady's arrival.

Another visitor was my uncle Ivek, Joe's half-brother. I can't say for sure I ever saw the man completely sober. He drank first thing in the morning when he poured šljivovica into his coffee, then throughout the rest of the day as he drank one gemišt after another, although this impression of insobriety came partly from his manner of speech, the stones in his mouth, as Mila had said. Ivek showed up in his cement mixer which he drove for the factory in Rakitje called *Tempo*. Even though perhaps he wasn't totally sober, he drove that thing with skill, which prompted his daughter, another Željka, to remark proudly to me once that her father "never had an accident, not one. He was an excellent driver!" The other thing I remember about Ivek was that he was missing his right index finger. The story about the finger was that he'd lost it in the military sawing wood on a stand-up saw. This was around 1960 and he was about to start his two-year service. The authorities began an investigation into whether he'd mutilated himself on purpose to avoid duty, but in the end concluded that his injury was exactly what it seemed at first glance—an accident.

He came to Srebrnjak just before lunch, around one in the afternoon. Štefek was back to normal, and both he and Mila were relaxed and friendly. They seemed happy to have Ivek there, and why not—he was one of the boys from long ago. He was family. They talked about people they knew, who'd died recently, what so-and-so was doing. Ivek lived in Rakitje and wasn't up on any news about people around here, so Mila told him what she knew from that telepathic peasant wire she got gossip from. Štefek kept filling Ivek's glass of wine, adding a little water too (he didn't drink himself), and sat there after lunch in no special hurry to get back out there. That was the other thing I remember about Ivek's visit—Štefek's not especial hurry to return to work. Maybe he was just sleepy after Ivek's soporific speech; it was hard work trying to figure out what the hell he was saying!

After lunch, Ivek drove me in his cement mixer to a café bar up in the hills. There were other cafés closer by, but he picked one at the summit of a hill on the road towards Sveti Martin pod Okićem. From there, we could gaze down at the surrounding valleys and the wide plain to the west where the town of Samobor twinkled orange in the distance. It was really something to sit up high in that cement mixer and drive along those narrow country roads across which the odd chicken would race idiotically just as that big truck ploughed along, and really something to see Ivek handle every corner like a professional even though he'd had multiple gemišt in Srebrnjak. The café was spare in the communist way, with metal chairs and a large photo of Tito above the bar. Men wearing blue tunics who had finished work for the day were drinking beer, and Ivek and I sat by the window with a nice view of the cement truck. I can picture us there now, drinking beer and trying to communicate, me expressing myself in my newly learned but improving Croatian, he talking with stones in his mouth, so that in the end he might have understood me better than I him. But he was full of good will; he had really nothing else to offer me other than this time together, and I am always happy he took me with him and that we had this brief memorable bonding at a bar in the hills above Srebrnjak.

Due to a lack of men on hand one afternoon, I was asked to hold down a pig's leg for its slaughter. Normally pigs were killed every fall, but this summer Jana and Dragec had run out of meat. I don't remember if I knew all day that I was to help, or whether it was a last-minute thing, but I have a clear image in my mind of Dragec in the yard sharpening the knives on a grinding stone that he turned with a foot pedal. He took great care with the long blade.

When the hour approached, Željka went for a walk. "I hate the sound," she said, "it is one of the most terrible things to hear." She paused, then added, with a smirk, "but I like pork chops!"

Jana gave me a pair of work pants and old leather shoes, which were too big, and in which my feet swam around. The place chosen to slaughter the pig was in the narrow space between the outdoor kitchen and the woodpile that ran parallel with it. The front door of the pigsty led straight out into that space. Dragec, Milivoj, Miško, and I waited while Jana opened the door and coaxed the pig out with some bread or grain she'd strewn on the concrete. The pig came out hesitatingly and blinking against the sharp light of the day like a prisoner that had been locked up in dark solitary confinement. It was a big animal, 150 kilos. Uncertain, suspicious. It seemed to presage dimly something bad about to happen to it but couldn't resist the food. Pigs are smart but they never learn. At a gesture from Dragec we were on it. Milivoj and Miško used their weight to heave it on its side and I held a back leg as the pig bucked ferociously and squealed in terror. The sound was like a saw grinding through rusty metal. It bucked under our knees, its ears flapping around, eyes popping out. Dragec tied up its snout with a rope that he'd already tied in a noose, the most precarious moment for him, then when he was ready for Jana to hand him the knife, she was nowhere to be found. He started screaming—What the hell was she waiting for? Maybe the priest to deliver the last rites?—and when I looked up I saw her lying on the ground on her back, the knife beside her. She struggled to her feet and handed Dragec the knife. He drove the blade in, and the squeal rose to a crescendo that finally gurgled out and lapped red against my shoes. Jana had tripped on a shovel that stuck out of the woodpile. Now, after some bickering with Dragec, she sat on a stool by the outdoor kitchen, wiping a tear away and holding her back. The pig lay there, massive and silent. I stood not moving, my heart beating hard.

Jana couldn't sit there any longer because there was still work to do. The pots of boiling water on her stove had to be emptied into the large cast-iron tub in the middle of the yard, into which we were going to put the pig, and it was going to be scraped of its hairs and cleaned. So back and forth she went, with Miško pouring in the water. Then we lifted the pig and placed it in the tub. There were two chains across the tub so that the pig could later be lifted out of the water cleanly. "Don't just drop it," Dragec warned us. After they'd cleaned the body, they hung it upside down on chains from hooks that were embedded in the concrete roof above the outdoor table, and Dragec slit open the belly so the guts fell out in a purple-blue bunch, which he cut out and put in a pail, some of which would be used for sausage casings, some thrown to the cats in the field behind the barn, and some of it thrown away. There was the business of cutting up the pig on the table by the outdoor kitchen—the same table where we'd sat after haying, with Dragec giving orders and Miško giving back directions, and Milivoj, the biggest man there, just following along. The blood was collected to make sausages, and the fat piled together for lard and fried fat bits called *čvarci*. By then I'd kicked off my shoes, which were soaked with blood, put my gloves on the wood pile, and went to shower. I wanted to get the smell off my body. Afterwards, the smell was off me, but when I came back down it was still heavy in the air as the men worked, and only the next day, after Jana used a corn broom and water on the concrete, and the night dew freshened the air, did it finally go away.

During this period, I explored the area beyond Srebrnjak and Dol, hopping onto the black girl's bike that had once belonged to Štefek's younger daughter, and that he sometimes rode to pick up supplies from the store like salt or sugar or flour, stacking them on the front handlebar. I rode to the bottom of Srebrnjak then turned left towards Sveta Nedelja, a large village with two churches, a school, graveyard, grocery store, and some café bars. Before Sveta Nedelja, I passed through the hamlet of Brezje. There, in somewhat ramshackle houses, lived the Ratković clan. The Ratkovići had a bad reputation among people in the area because they were poor and slovenly and were just generally considered to be "trash." A few of their younger children were playing on the side of the road, some of them barefoot and in underwear. A young woman was roller-skating a hundred metres farther on. I assumed she belonged to the Ratković family, though my first thought when I saw her up close dispelled that possibility. She didn't look like anyone around here. Her blonde curls, fair skin, now a honey-coloured in mid-summer, and her green almond-shaped eyes and high cheek bones gave her the look of a misplaced gem in the wilderness. She was also cold and standoffish, so that now looking back I don't think she said a word to me.

In English I began, "Nice evening, eh?" sounding to myself, not for the last time, like an American parody of a Canadian. "Do you live nearby?" No answer. Just skating along. "Do you know English?" I asked. I was under the impression that speaking a foreign language to girls from around here was a big advantage, a sort of distinguishing mark. She gave me a searing, contemptuous look that clearly said "Fuck off." When English didn't work, I tried German, my first language. But nothing. So that was that. I got back on my bike and went on to Sveta Nedelja. I felt chastened, sure, but also proud of myself for having for once followed through on the advice Joe first gave me long ago in Maui when he urged me to approach the girl in the orange bikini.

Two days later, I drove to Brezje again and again saw the girl on the road, this time just walking along. Even though I have no memory of it (just a memory of being rejected the first time!), we had a conversation, then another one a few days later, and then made plans to go on a walk to the Marija Magdalena chapel. Teodora Hictaler was her name, Tea as she called herself. Her last name sounded Austrian or German (*taler* or *thaler* being the old German currency), so perhaps her ancestors had been officials in the Austro-Hungarian empire that controlled Croatia in the nineteenth century. Her English turned out to be better than anyone's I'd yet met in the country, totally without an accent, yet she had grown up in Brezje in a little shack by the road with two illiterate peasants who had been given a stipend by the Yugoslav government to raise her. Not right off but later, she told me, "I never knew my father, and my mother was just fifteen when she had me, and too young and immature to take care of me properly. Actually, she was always too immature, even when she was a grown woman. And she became an alcoholic also. She visited me here when I was eight or nine, then afterwards maybe once a year. It was always strange. I felt uncomfortable with this strange person who was my mother. Once, I was still very young, she sat outside our house here under the trees, and every few minutes went inside to the bathroom with her purse. As the afternoon went on, she started to change. Her face got redder and more swollen. She acted strangely. That's all the little girl that was me knew. Now I know she had liquor in her purse and was drinking secretly in the bathroom. It was terrible!"

On the day of our walk I went down the Srebrnjak road to meet Tea as she walked up from Brezje. She was accompanied by her thirteen-year-old cousin who was visiting. She said he followed her everywhere that summer, like a puppy. That was okay; I wasn't disappointed, this wasn't a date exactly, nor was he a gooseberry. Yet her face and those curls, the melody in her voice and her mysterious, somehow tragic presence, left me with an afterglow every time I looked at her.

The three of us climbed the gravel road to the Marija Magdalena chapel. We met no one on the way up. It was very quiet. Swallows darted around telegraphing messages with their flights. The ochre chapel was unlocked so we went inside and, for some reason, jokingly, said a few pretend vows. She told me her grandmother, the woman who had taken care of her for the first years of her life when her mother was unable to, had recently died, and that I was saving her. As we walked back home, the cousin took her hand and placed it in mine. We went down to the bottom of the Srebrnjak road, walking hand in hand. And then we said goodbye.

I saw Tea two more times that summer. I saw her once on the road to Dol with her next door friend, Natalija, a girl three years younger, so sixteen, whose black curly hair made her seem altogether the opposite of Tea, whom I met only this one time and knew nothing about. I couldn't have known, as she could not have known, the direction her life was going to go, so that when I think of her now as I write and know her story, and see her smiling and happy on this walk with Tea, I want to reach out and shake her and tell her to wake up, tell her she can still turn it around and stay away from all those men. The second time I saw Tea was on the same road, with Natalija again, this time from my vantage point of Vlado's bedroom window where I was spending time with Željka, listening to his LPs. When I saw the two girls approaching the house at the crossroads, I moved from the window and let them go past. It turned out they were going to Srebrnjak to see me. When they neared the yard of the house an old woman, Željka's grandmother, Strina Slava, heard them ask for me and, without a word, turned around and went inside and shut the door on them.

Coda Yugoslavia + Rab

When my mother took a sabbatical in Paris, we visited Yugoslavia as a family again. It was the last time we would ever do so because within in a year my parents would separate. Miško later said, shaking his head wistfully, "So the dynasty has come to an end." It never occurred to me until now that our family fell apart around the same time as Yugoslavia itself.

It is apt then that in this period of breaking apart my grandmother, Joe's mother, made an appearance in Srebrnjak. Draga Husta showed up like some character out of a book I had read and had brought to life but never expected to see in the flesh. She was wearing black clothes and a black kerchief because of the recent death of her husband, Husta. She was a tall woman with a loud, windy personality that blew heavily through the little kitchen in Srebrnjak. I was told she had been good-looking in her youth, but I had trouble imagining that when I looked at her sagging, somewhat masculine face with its large jaw and fleshy nose and dark, not exactly friendly eyes. Her reason for visiting Srebrnjak as opposed to us going to Molvice as we had in 1977, where she lived with her husband and two stepsons—one with whom she was alleged to have had an affair; the other a hunchback called Jura who conscientiously watched over my sister and me when we were put astride the heavy horse—was because Joe had decided never to go to Molvice again on a visit. So, there she was in Srebrnjak. How long had it been since she'd seen Strina or Mila I don't know. Likely decades. They had lived in the same little peasant house for four years, but after her marriage and departure there had been no reason to communicate. She didn't seem nervous at all. However, with every passing minute, the atmosphere in the kitchen got more uncomfortable, the oxygen more sucked out of it, and Joe more paralyzed, sitting on his chair not talking, abject and stiff. Luckily, Miško was there to take up the conversational slack; he was the only one who said anything really, engaging her about this and that— her health, the upcoming crops. Mila, I remember, said a few words of greeting when Draga Husta arrived, invited her to sit, but beyond that didn't offer much in the way of conversation, and watched instead the spectacle unfold from a voyeuristic distance, slyly enjoying the awful uncomfortableness of it all. Strina Slava was on her wooden box, but beyond Draga Husta's attention, as though she were inconsequential. They were total opposites in personality, these two women, and the best and least selfish of the two was the meekest and most invisible. I wish I'd asked Strina what she thought, but I never did. Draga Husta ignored my mother too for the most part and, thinking she knew no Croatian, disparaged her with the observation that she looked like a little girl. My mother, who had understood her, piped up, "Well I am not a little girl!" (On the issue of the size of my mother, who was just over five feet tall, I'm reminded of a story she told me about her stay back in 1969, when she showed some outsized moxie by daring the people in Srebrnjak to sing the (then) "discouraged" *Lijepa naša domovina*, the Croatian anthem, which they did. She also took it upon herself, when she heard that Štefek and his father had not spoken in two decades, to go over to the old man's house and, with hand gestures and faltering Croatian, invite him over for lunch.)

I too was outside the scope of my grandmother's attention. I don't think she spoke to me other than "hello" and "goodbye." Even that I'm not sure about. I'd been told by Jana that I resembled my grandfather, that is, Draga Husta's first husband, so maybe that put her off. I don't know. In hindsight, I've become more charitable towards her and her visit to Srebrnjak and have subsumed it within a bigger picture of her possible remorse for the past, thinking that she wished she could have chosen a different path, had it over again to do differently—a wish covered up by her bluster, loudness, and self-centredness. Or, contrariwise, maybe the way she behaved in Srebrnjak was exactly who she always was. Yet, even as I say that I remember Joe telling me she did have a selfless side because she made sure her sons were legally titled to the land in Srebrnjak upon her marriage and because she had been on a local committee after the Second World War, which helped saved the life of Štefek's younger brother, who had been arrested by the Partisans and probably would have been hanged had she and the committee not convinced a local commander that seventeen-year-old Miško was innocent, was a nobody without political interests.

Skyping with Joe this afternoon as I write this story, he denies she ever asked him to come to Canada, which I assumed was part of her reason for visiting that afternoon, denies her regret and remorse, denies she asked him from her sick bed one last time before she died, wailing loudly as though he were on the other side of the house. I have a memory of this happening, and even wrote about it in my first book. During our conversation, he says, "Why the fuck would she do that? She wasn't stupid, you know. She knew what the answer was going to be."

Joe didn't want to talk about her anymore. I could see it on his face. Suddenly serious, sombre, petulant even, poking at his teeth with a toothpick. "I'm going to tell you this slowly so you never forget it," he said. "So listen. I was four, and she came to Srebrnjak to visit us; she didn't come after that. When she left, I followed her to the top of the hill, right over here, where my father's vineyard used to be. I asked her to take me with her. She gave me twenty dinars. I will never forget it. She gave me twenty dinars to go home. To get rid of me. The money was useless; it had no fucking meaning to me, nothing. I watched her go on. And I went back home. I gave Mila the money because I didn't have any use for it." He stopped talking. There was nothing else. Even now, seventy years later, that incident with his mother was like an old wound that still hurt inside, a scab that was still raw underneath.

To me, the meeting with Draga Husta lingers more powerfully now than it did when it happened. As uncomfortable as it must have been for Joe, her visit to Srebrnjak, which brought back all the bad feelings of that scene on the hill, was for me just an awkward and unpleasant encounter of second intensity.

My own experiences during that period were light by comparison. I went to Zagreb several times to see a movie or just to experience the city. Željka and I rode to Sveta Nedelja and left our bikes inside the yard of a family she knew, caught a bus for the Ljubljanica station, and from there rode a tram to the centre of town, the *Trg Republike* (Republic Square).

The centre of Zagreb had been refurbished for the 1987 University Games, so its newly painted pastel façades and paving showed off well even at night. Hundreds of young people were strolling through the streets, many of them university-educated, culturally sophisticated, and well travelled in Europe (Tito had long before loosened travel restrictions). By then I'd met Vlado's fellow medical students, like Hrvoj ("Harvey" I called him) whose parents had gifted him their apartment somewhere in the concrete wasteland of new Zagreb and where we listened to his record collection, especially the

Doors' first album and his favourite band, Colosseum, and drank Stari Zagreb beer. Vlado had a decent record collection, much of it produced by the record label Jugoton, which was based in Zagreb but distributed throughout Yugoslavia and that had signed the biggest acts in Yugo rock and popular music, like Azra, Bijelo Dugme (White Button), Crvena Jabuka (Red Apple), Đorđe Balašević, to name just a few. An irony of my relationship with Yugo rock was that I never listened to much of it while I was in Yugoslavia, but only on YouTube years later when the country was dead, in the heart of the snowy Newfoundland winter. As I write this, the Bijelo Dugme ballad I listened to the other night comes to me, "Evo, zakleču se—Here, I'll swear," "Hey, carry this song one last time / To a street by the river / Forever forbidden / Except for my steps. / Hey, if someone could carry an olive branch / To one door, / A door I forever closed / A long, long time ago. . . ."

In Zagreb's lively evening atmosphere, through the streets filled with people, we went to an old movie house, Željka and I, to see Wim Wenders' *Paris, Texas*. It was the only film I ever saw in Yugoslavia or in Croatia and it left a lasting impression because I ended up teaching it when I got my first contract. The film tells the story of a passionate but jealous husband and his young, beautiful, at first naive wife, their violent breakup, and his redemption at the end. The story of extreme love and violent jealousy really didn't square with any of my own tepid and jejune experiences up to that stage. Maybe that was still to come, but on this evening it left me wrapped in a thoughtful, sweetly bitter mood.

My bike ride home that evening with Željka was benign and unremarkable, yet pleasant and memorable nonetheless. Talking and laughing, we rode side-by-side in and out of the pools of lights from the streetlamps. Crickets were chirping in the freshly mowed fields. The warm air smelled sweetly of the grass. When we arrived at her place, we went into the kitchen to eat the smoked ham, boiled eggs and bread Jana had left for us. Upstairs we played a few hands of poker, a game I'd introduced to her that summer. Afterwards, I headed back to Srebrnjak. It was one in the morning.

I struggled those first few seconds in the saddle. The light on Štefek's bike, powered by the generator on the wheel, shone feebly onto the road ahead of me. My sleepiness wore off, though, when I hit the gravel road in Srebrnjak. I was wide awake then. I knew that up ahead Tomo's gate was going to be open. Tomo was a farmer just down the road from Štefek; an old school friend of Joe's—the two of them used to go out chasing girls back in the day. I knew Tomo's dogs would be unchained and roaming free. During the day, Tomo's gate was shut and his dogs used to race wickedly along its length when I passed by on my bike. I had no doubt they would have attacked me had the gate not been there. Štefek himself had told me that one of Tomo's dogs had bit him on the ankle once—not nipped, no, actually bit him. Besides, my recent bad experience with a German Shepherd guard dog on a boat in Toronto was fresh in my mind. At night, Tomo loosed his dogs, two of them for sure, maybe three, and left his gate wide open. Why he did that I don't know. I guess he wanted to free them because they were locked up during the day. He didn't expect anyone to pass by after a certain hour. But a part of me wondered whether a punitive morality made him free his dogs. He was deciding you had no business passing there at night or must be up to no good if you chose to do so and would sure as hell face his dogs. So that is why I wasn't sleepy anymore as I drove up the Srebrnjak road. I'd gone past Tomo's before and had narrowly escaped. This time I could vaguely descry the menacing shapes of the dogs ahead of me, darker than the road itself, like black phantoms. It was almost worse seeing them wait for me than being surprised by them as I rode past. I took an emergency circuitous route off the road and into the field on the left and around the back of one of the houses and then back onto the road again. Things might have turned out a lot worse for me had I slowed there and not been able to outrace the dogs, but that didn't occur to me at the time. They didn't notice me, it turned out. Or had noticed me but didn't go beyond their territory. When I leaned the bike against the closed barn at home and found the key on the window ledge and entered the kitchen, my heart was still beating fast.

That summer in Srebrnjak ended with one final get together of our extended family for a pig roast. Among those attending were my half-uncle Ivek, snazzily dressed in a blue polyester shirt and brown slacks, and his wife Luba, a pretty but by then rotund and sedentary woman who'd sewn my parents a blue table cloth with white checks similar to the Croatian *šahovnica* (Coat of Arms) that I still use for Christmas now; also at the pig roast was Mila and Jana's other sister, Draga, an attractive dark-haired woman with large, sad eyes who was soft on her twenty-something-year-old son, Božo, who was in his element that afternoon with the wine and his guitar. Also at the roast was Božo's father, Draga's husband, the chain-smoking politically savvy Ivek Krajačić with his white hair slicked back and his suave gravelly voice that made me think that the rumours of his infidelity must have been true or at least possible. It was he who long ago had carved chess pieces out of a willow tree and gifted them to my father. Miško had been in Srebrnjak the whole day, working. He had helped my father and Štefek prepare the pig, tying its feet with wire and impaling it on the wooden spit, and he'd turned the pig for long stretches. When finally he took a break out front of the house with my mother, who was sitting in the shade reading African literature for an essay she was writing, he questioned her, as he had me, about this intellectual business of hers, so that she dismissed him with a click of her tongue, which she did when she was annoyed, and then carried on because she wasn't going to argue with a driving instructor who hadn't read a thing in his life. My sister Natasha was there too—sweet sixteen, slim and dark-haired, her brown hair nicely coiffed, having just come from Paris where my mother had been on sabbatical. My sister, who resembled Joe and moved shyly around, not talking much, who would help me that summer secretly empty my mother's Dalmane capsules and put flour inside instead to prove she could sleep without them. Even Jana and Dragec had left their work at home and had come to Srebrnjak for a few hours.

After our meal, after the dessert of strudel, *kremšnita*, and Turkish coffee, Božo pulled out his guitar and they sang some songs. Even Štefek joined in. He had a good voice and had been known to enjoy singing. This was the first and only time I ever heard him. He was flushed in the face, not from the wine that he didn't drink anymore, but from some feeling that brought the colour out, and I see him still, sitting at the head of the table, his back to all that work for an hour, for an hour at least.

Then my mother herded everyone together for a photo-graph. Presciently, it seemed, she sensed that this extended family would never be together again. When she was about to snap the picture, however, she noticed that Štefek had dis-appeared. He had gone to the barn to deal with the cows. We could hear him swearing at them for sitting in their dung. He didn't come out, maybe because he was busy or just because he thought a photograph was frivolous. So now when I look at the photo, I don't see him there. What I see is the photo of us together one last time, much younger, many dead now, but alive then and in a good mood and happy.

On that last family trip to Yugoslavia, we travelled to the coast to wrap up our stay. It was our first vacation on the sea since our trip to Brač in 1977. And it would be our last together. We were going to another island, Rab, farther north than Brač in the Kvarner region of the Adriatic.

The road to the coast took us first through Kordun and Lika, a sparsely populated area, past Plitvice Lakes, a six-kilometre-long chain of sixteen turquoise lakes and numerous waterfalls in deep woods, then through wide rolling grasslands where white stones poked from the earth and sheep, whose shepherds used to guide them north in the spring and return later in the summer, grazed. The road reached the mountainous coastal interior and eventually ascended steeply in hard turns before it sheared through the last rock and descended to the Adriatic.

On this road during the Yugoslav years, school kids from the north were driven to the sea for holidays. As one former student told me, "Plitvice was an important stop on all those treks: not for the natural beauty, but because of the bathroom stop. Everybody had to pee by the time the bus came up in Plitvice." The kids would "barf all the way up those hills" as they crossed the Velebit Mountains, but all would be forgotten once they reached the sea.[6]

The landscape of Lika is wooded and hilly in places, open and empty in others. I saw an occasional brick farmhouse with its straw ricks and fruit orchards and peasant women sitting at tables under umbrellas selling jars of honey and large discs of cheese. Outside *gostionice*, the local roadhouses, pigs and sheep turned on spits in giant cast-iron barbecues and modern folk music floated out from the speakers. We sat on the veranda at one such place and as we ate, we looked out at the land around, a big flat space of dry grass bordered in the distance by low grey mountains that rippled from the heat off the highway. I liked the area, but I could also see that it didn't offer much of a future to an imaginative and ambitious person, like the inventor Nikola Tesla, who was born in nearby Smiljan.

A Yugoslav flag hung outside the gostionica, but I noticed some stickers of the Croatian flag with its checkerboard šahovnica on a light pole by the road. These were the last

---

6 Thanks to Renata Schellenberg for these observations.

days of Yugoslavia. During that time, the dinar plummeted. I remember buying groceries with a 1,000-dinar bill and a few months later needing a 100,000 bill. (That increasingly useless 1,000-dinar bill aptly depicted a way of life and ideology that was fading too; it showed a communist-style image of a young peasant woman in a kerchief presenting grapes on her open palm, along with a corn cob, an apple, and other products of the "diligent" Yugoslavian farmer). In August 1990, militant ethnic Serbs around Knin and other areas of the Krajina district, hard on the Bosnian border, protested the new nationalist Croatian government and barricaded roads leading to Dalmatia with logs (an event mockingly dubbed the "log revolution" by Croatian media). But few Croats realized that these laughable "Balkan primitives" would help set in motion the war in Croatia and seize one third of its territory by the mid-90s. I knew little about all of this at the time, though when a Serbian clerk refused me, a Canadian with a Croatian last name, a boarding pass on a JAT flight from Toronto to Zagreb in 1990 because I didn't have a visa, something routinely granted on arrival, and that he had no authority to demand, I see in hindsight how enmity between Serbs and Croats was already building.

My stay in Toronto as a result of missing my flight was an eventful one. At the airport I met a Croatian Canadian by a row of pay phones in the departure hall and, hearing him speak Croatian, I struck up a conversation with him. Ivan Kačić took me in for two nights, fed me and showed me around Toronto. This tour included a Croatian-owned ferry boat in the harbour, where, when the cooks in the kitchen said we could go freely to the third level of the ship, I was attacked by a German Shepherd guard dog as soon as I stepped through the door. It rushed at me and bit me in the leg. I had just enough time to back out the door and slam it shut. The cooks smiled slyly as we came back down. Ivan drove me to the hospital for a shot. The next day we went to the Yugoslavian embassy to buy a visa and Ivan did most of the talking to the Serbian clerk, all of it in English. In the end I paid five bucks and got a sticker in my passport, which is what I had always received when I used to arrive in Zagreb.

On our last trip to the coast together, my family and I drove through the area just before the roads became impassable. After Gospić and the hills of Ličko Polje, we crossed the Velebit Mountains through a pass aptly named *Oštarijska vrata* (Dangerous Doors). Like most roads across the Velebit range, this one drills between serrated white limestone crags and wrenches cars left and right as it climbs and descends. Once over the top I was able to enjoy the long view of sloping, rocky meadows and slim white strips of barren islands and then, finally, at the limit of where my eyes could reach, the open Adriatic. The dark blue sea melted into the sky. Sunshine spread warmly on the crisp fresh air. The feeling that came over me was the same one I would have year after year, that I'd left behind the ordinary all too-human world of the earth and had arrived instead in the land of the gods. It was a feeling of elation, a moment of breathless pause before the clean lines and pure air of sea and islands and sky.

Soon after, we were sailing to Rab on a Jadrolinija car ferry. My mood was high, but when I first saw Rab, its white, rocky, desolate carapace rearing out of the sea, I was disappointed. The island didn't seem worth visiting.

Half an hour later we were driving inland where I saw the country change. The stone-pocked fields were now sprinkled with a yellow herb with a curry aroma which I misheard one woman tell me was *bosilje*, basil, but which I discovered years later was *smilje*, a form of everlasting, or immortelle. I saw junipers, olive and fig orchards, low-growing vineyards covered by the dust from the roads, and pens for goats and sheep. There were new white-washed villas with balconies and vine gazebos. Villas and housing complexes were everywhere.

The island of the 1930s that Rebecca West describes in *Black Lamb and Grey Falcon* was a rather different one. "[H]igh up on the bare mountains. . . [are] olive terraces; in the valleys there are olive terraces; in the trough of the valleys there are walled fields where an ordinary crop of springing corn or grass strikes one as an abnormal profusion like a flood. On these enclosures black figures work frenetically. From a grey sky reflected light pours down and makes of every terrace and field a stage on which these black figures play each their special drama of toil, of frustration, of anguish. As we passed by on the stony causeway, women looked up at us, from the fields, their faces furrowed with all known distresses."[7]

However, on my trip to Rab I didn't see the numerous olive terraces, nor the indigent peasants mentioned by West. Rab's natural vegetation had covered over this past. Later, though, I saw an abandoned house or two in the hills above the main road that hinted at the difficulties people had trying to make a life on Rab. One was notable for its size and presence, standing empty, but regally, above the world around it, with its balconies and well-wrought cornices, an extension of the people who once owned it and might have left Rab at the end of the nineteenth century when phylloxera (vine lice) infested the islands and decimated the wine industry, or who had escaped during the Yugoslav years. Inside were castoff items like old boots and personal letters, stained and crumbling, best wishes from a family member already far away.

Now, at the start of this visit to Rab, I got out of the car and looked around at the country. Nimble black birds flew past and whistled in the bushes. Patches of bay leaf clustered along dusty brick-hard paths that crisscrossed the hills, and a faint scent of rosemary and thyme was now mixed with the curry-like herb that had blown into the open windows of my car and

---

7 Rebecca West, *Black Lamb and Grey Falcon: A Journey through Yugoslavia* (New York: The Viking Press, 1941), 132.

was blowing across the island. I put a sprig of the stuff in my camera bag, and when I opened it months later, the smell was still there, which took me right back to the island.

The old man waved me up the concrete steps to the seat across from him, then called over the café owner, a paunchy guy wearing gold chains and rings and a big-collared, flowery shirt. "You from Kanada?" the owner asked. He spoke English with a thick accent. When I answered in the affirmative, he filled three shot glasses with šljivovica. We knocked them in a toast and downed them.

"No charge," he said, waving aside my money. He brought out another bottle that said "Zadarski Maraschino" on the label. He filled the shot glasses again, this time with a hard liquor that had a sweetish cherry flavour. The two shots warmed me pleasantly. It was around nine in the morning on a windless sunny day. From the café on the promenade that wound along the coast to the town of Rab, around two kilometres distant, I could see a little sandy beach, already crowded. Two guys were playing a game called *picigin*, tossing a small rubber ball around in the shallow water.

My host, who had lived in Mississauga in the 1970s, had run this business for ten years. He wanted to expand but was discouraged by restrictions imposed by the Yugoslav government. "I give example: I want bring Warsteiner for my German guests, but too many taxes, red tape, so I no can. They put me in situation I have no choice." Hands up, shrugging. He said he was fed up with the country. It was time for Croatia to be independent. However, he didn't know whether that would ever happen in his lifetime. He was hopeful, but not optimistic.

When I went to Rab next, Yugoslavia would be no more, and Croatia would be a new nation, but for now it was still Yugoslavia, though of course it had always been Rab no matter who governed it. I asked them about how they thought of themselves, as islanders first or as Croatians.

"Well you know," my host answered, speaking in Croatian now, "that depends, and it's different for some people. For me I come from Rab, this is home, but I am a Croat you better believe it. Not everyone who lives here was born on the island. I would say I'm a citizen of Rab, but not exactly an island nationalist."

"Look, it's like this," the old man said, "this here is the mainland, and that over there is an island. Where we are is always the centre, if you follow me."

He wagged a thick finger. "This is the most beautiful island in all of Croatia. You got a lot to see." Looking across the bay at Rab's shimmering walls jutting like a prow into the sea, I couldn't imagine he was wrong. "We have everything," he went on, using his fingers to list the items, "we have the sea, we have good food, we have a beautiful town, another Dubrovnik. . . ."

"What about the other islands?" I wondered.

"Every island has qualities," replied the owner. "They are all different. Each one has a special flavour. But in his opinion Rab is the best."

"And not in yours?" the old man asked.

"Sure, in mine too."

"Good. Now let's have another one," he said, pointing at the bottle.

"He can have another one. You've had enough. Besides, you owe me."

I thanked him but declined. I said goodbye and made my way to town.

Walking from the east, I circumnavigated the marina, which in the summer was jammed white with skiffs, small motorboats, and the occasional sailboat, though no grand yachts as there would be a few years later. I went into the oldest section of Rab, Kaldanac. Rab is built on a rising peninsula of stone pointing into the bay of Sveta Fumija (Saint Euphemia).

The cream-coloured, neatly fitted flagstones of the main street, named in those days after Yugoslav Partisan youth hero Ivo Lola Ribar, were perpendicular to strings of smaller streets, many paved smooth with stone or patches of concrete of the same hue. The lower section of town nearest the marina was the most active, with the usual cafés, restaurants and shops selling jewellery, clothing, wooden *furnir* (scenes of the town built out of little bits of wood) and engraved wooden bowls. Farther up, on the other side of town, were the main churches, including the four bell towers.

I left the main street and took a crooked alley to this quiet section of Rab. Not yet noon, a few locals were out taking care of business, and some windows were open so I could hear the voices of people inside, but otherwise I was alone. Arrows of sunlight slanted down the lengths of the main streets or collected in pools in little corners. As the sun moved across the sky, more and more of the town was in the shade. Looking at a map, I noticed that most of Rab's main streets avoid the longitudinal rays of the sun's worst heat. I came to this quarter in other years, later in the afternoon, and it was always shady and cool in comparison to the world outside. And quiet as a church, which is appropriate since there are around half a dozen of them along the western wall.

From a high point on the northwestern side of town, I could see Rab's four campaniles rise cleanly from the ruffled irregularity of the tiled roofs. The church of Sveta Justina (Saint Justine), now the Museum of Sacred Art, is said to contain the gold-plated reliquary of the skull of Saint Christopher that was brought to Rab by an eleventh-century bishop during the period when the town was under attack by Sicilian Normans. Placed on the city walls, legend has it, Saint Christopher miraculously repulsed the invaders by changing the direction of the wind and driving their ships off to sea. Somewhat removed from the churches, appropriately as it turns out, was the palace of the Nimir and Dominis families, and the birthplace of Rab's most famous citizen, Markantun de Dominis (1560–1624). He was a Jesuit-educated natural scientist and theologian who explained the phenomenon of refraction in the workings of the rainbow, which was acknowledged by Newton, and who first proved the moon's influence on the tides. However, his independent and irascible personality vexed most of his later years. Promoted from bishop of Senj to archbishop of Split ("Spalato" in those years), he quarrelled with clergy, was excommunicated by his archdiocese, and departed for England, where he was warmly welcomed by James I. He stayed six years, railed against the Catholic Church in his ten-volume *De Republica Ecclesiastica*, and was named Dean of Windsor in 1619. But in England too his days were numbered as his relationship with authorities there (and even with the king) cooled off. Never wholly committed to Anglicanism and, concerned about his position due to changing political circumstances, he decided to return to Rome in 1622, counting on his benefactor, his relative Pope Gregory XV. Unluckily, for both the Pope and former archbishop, Gregory died in 1623, and de Dominis was imprisoned by the former's less sympathetic successor in a cell without windows in the Castel Sant'Angelo. When he died his body was burned in the Camp dei Fiori, along with copies of his writings.

I descended steep stairs to a walkway beneath Rab's western walls. Sunlight was just peeking over the roofs and onto the promenade, still moist with dew, and onto the narrow inlet. The sea was light turquoise near shore and a dark cyan in deeper places. The smoothly polished surface of the water undulated gently. It was very quiet. Only the voices of a few elderly people, who had placed their towels on tiny beaches between the stones or on the walkway itself, disturbed the silence.

This was the spot my grandmother, Oma, visited in 1938. I know because of a black-and-white photo of her I found half a century after she had been to Rab. It was dated 1 June 1938.

She is sitting against some stones on this promenade, relaxed and smiling, dressed in black pants and white blouse. I recognize her face, her hair, though it is not the face of the woman I knew. She is accompanied by two girlfriends and three local men who happened to stop by. The photographer saw them together and snapped the picture. The photo of Oma itself doesn't speak very much but the evidence of her presence here long before mine is haunting, our meeting of sorts across time that neither of us could have imagined, indirect and accidental. I'm able to look back at her but she can't see me. What was she talking about as she sat there? Did they leave together, the three couples, ascending the very same stairs I had just come down? What happened then? The identity of the elderly woman who took care of me as a boy—who picked me up from school at lunch and made me potato pancakes and read German magazines in the summer shade of her west Edmonton house and fell asleep watching The National with her head back, mouth open, snoring—began to change. Another woman, a young woman with another life, suddenly appeared through the photograph.

On that trip to Rab I didn't know any of this yet. I was in my own moment. I picked a spot between boulders to put my things and slipped into the sea. With three or four strokes I broke the green glassy surface of the still water and got part way across the channel. Looking down, below my feet, I saw black fish slide past in tubular formations. There must have been sounds too, the putter of an outboard from a boat taking tourists somewhere, bells from the high towers tolling, but I couldn't hear them. All I remember is looking around me, seeing Rab's high stone walls, sun golden, and Rab's towers rising above the rest of the stone city that pointed into the blue Adriatic as though it were setting out on a voyage.

Srebrnjak Winter

When I flew into Zagreb in December 1992, I saw the ominous, disconcerting sight of hundreds of crows huddled in a huge black mass on the far side of the tarmac. They had gathered against the cold and the snow and from time to time they rose en masse and landed somewhere else. Yugoslavia was dead and a new Croatia had been born. The "log revolution" in Knin in 1990, which had seemed comedic at first, had turned very serious. Propaganda directed at Serbs inside Croatia about the allegedly imminent threat of the new nationalist Croatian government, led by Franjo Tuđman, fomented rebellion and war. Vukovar fell in 1991. A third of Croatian territory was seized by Serb-led paramilitaries supported by the Yugoslav National Army (JNA, Jugoslavenska narodna armija). The war in Croatia would spread even more violently in Bosnia-Herzegovina.

So, it seemed a natural time to go on a holiday to Croatia, or at least that was the conclusion reached by Joe. No one besides him thought it was a good idea. I was halfway through my Ph.D. at the University of New Brunswick in Fredericton by then, and classmates thought I was crazy for going. "You're crazy," one of them told me, a young guy with curly black hair who tried to impress me by telling me his habit every January of not drinking in order to prove to himself he wasn't an alcoholic at the age of twenty-one. "I mean you're going into a war zone! You have to ask yourself one question—do I feel lucky? Well, do you?"

Joe himself had reasons to go to Croatia in the middle of a war. Being with his Croatian family was, I think, a means of grounding himself again after his separation. Every morning he came down to the kitchen of the Srebrnjak house wearing a silk suit, silk tie and pointy leather shoes as though he were going out to a formal dinner. One suit was a shiny silver that glistened in the light, and one tie, which he wore without a trace of inhibition, had a pattern of red and blue soap bubbles, and was garishly out of sync with his refined silk suits. However, he was confident and immune to my mockery. He spent most of his day in the kitchen, which smelled heavily of burning wood and food cooking on the stove, like žganci or smoked sausages or blood sausages or a piece of pork already in the oven for our midday meal, with a glass of wine in front of him.

Other than conversations with people in the house, Joe's only other entertainment was watching the news about the war, or whatever documentary was on about Croatian cultural practices like grandma so-and-so's cheese-making in Slavonia. There was a lot of this in the new Croatia. The language, culture and history of the country were bound up more than ever with national pride. I was told that people had rediscovered the Catholic Church, went more often to Sunday mass, christened their newborns again, etc.—things they had done during the communist period, true, but that now intensified. I didn't notice this emphasis on religion among the people in Srebrnjak but there was a great deal of focus on the war effort and the news broadcasts, which we all gathered around to watch on the grainy black-and-white TV.

The front was fifty kilometres south, in Karlovac. I hadn't heard any of the fighting nor was I afraid, even though I knew that some bombs had hit Zagreb in the early days of the war and there had been a few skirmishes at the nearby Yugoslav army barracks at one point. Croatia was re-armed after the JNA had confiscated all of its weapons in 1990, so the likelihood of war in Srebrnjak, so near the capital, was low. For me, the ordinariness of every day in Srebrnjak, my history there and all my good memories, made the chances of all that coming to an end seem impossible.

It was very cold at night, and the small wood-burning stove upstairs in the hallway didn't heat well, and I wore a toque, socks, and multiple layers of clothing to bed. When I took a pee, the steam rose from the toilet's basin. I dreaded having to sit on the cold ceramic. Every two days I got a bucket of dried corncobs and started a fire for a shower. If I made the fire strong enough there would be enough warm water in the morning to wash my hair. As I found out, it was a bad idea to use cold water to wash your hair in the winter in Srebrnjak. But the one aspect of our fortnight in Croatia that winter that I wished I could have changed from the get-go was having to share a bed with Joe. Talk about someone not being your first choice. One night, I had a bizarre experience of falling into a deep sleep and then dreaming, dreaming of a woman with me in bed, beautiful and enticing, but upon throwing my arm around her in an ecstasy of anticipation, something inside me woke me in a fright, and I realized I was hugging my father instead!

We hadn't rented a car for our stay. Even though Miško was willing to take us wherever we wanted to go, he worked all day and normally didn't arrive until the afternoon. Sometimes he showed up with a student in tow and drove us somewhere. Not having a car was significant because it kept us in the kitchen, the only heated room in the house, most of the day. This was bad for Joe because he drank too much, but it was good for me because it forced me into the hills on long walks.

For the first few days the brown valley with its spectral and skeletal trees was hard to adjust to. I was so accustomed to the green summer in Srebrnjak, and my eyes had to accommodate themselves to the sparseness of the country. I could see farther now that the leaves were gone. I saw things I hadn't noticed before, like an abandoned nineteenth-century house in the upper valley that had once belonged to wealthy landowners from Samobor. The familiar sounds of summer had disappeared. Instead there was mainly silence, broken now and again by a dog barking or someone chopping wood. Smoke from stoves going all day filled the crisp air. I saw the thin grey lines rising and unfurling from kitchen chimneys and from barns, in which people were distilling šljivovica. The frozen ground crunched under my boots, but when the temperature climbed just a few degrees the earth grew soft and my boots got heavy with brown clayish mud. There was a lot of this clay in the upper hills of the valley from the topsoil having washed down over the years. As I walked through the orchards, I saw perfectly preserved apples that had gone unnoticed on the cold ground. Squished on the road in the upper part of Srebrnjak, where water in the ditches still flowed from a spring somewhere, were speckled black and yellow salamanders.

FIGURE 8. The barn in Srebrnjak in winter

The big changes in the area since I'd been here last didn't have to do with the time of year, but with the arrival of capitalism in the new Croatia. This was most noticeable in the form of small stores that had popped up in the area. I remember my astonishment at the array of new enterprises, especially with the products on the shelves. When before you went into the state-owned stores—SAMA or NAMA—and walked down the aisle where there were shaving supplies, for example, you had a choice of Ralon or Pino Silvestre aftershave and little else, but now all of a sudden Gillette and you name it had made inroads. When before there was just Yugoslav beer, now there were other options like Heineken or Tuborg, not to mention foreign hard liquors like Jack Daniel's, Canadian Club, and the like. Other new businesses had sprung up, such as the stone and ceramic tile company on the highway towards Samobor that sold imported slabs from all over the world, and a chic marble-floored café in Brezje with ceiling mirrors and black steel furnishings—a total anomaly in the countryside.

As I write I'm reminded of an incident in this bar a few years later, which proved that the shiny arrival of new commerce hadn't yet changed the bad service one used to get in Yugoslavia. I'd shown up at the café one afternoon wearing a canvas safari hat I'd bought at Canadian Tire, which prompted the waitress, a tall raw-boned blonde, to ask as soon as I stepped inside, "Where did you come from, cowboy?" The beer she served me was already open; she'd removed the cap from the half-litre bottle, and when I took a sip, I noticed a plastic spoon inside. I put the bottle back on the table and looked at it for a moment as various thoughts went through my mind. Besides the waitress, who I later discovered was also the owner, I was the only person in the bar. I waved her over and pointed out the spoon in the beer. I asked for my money back, and she said, "Why should you get your money back when you drank from this beer?" I told her I had only taken a sip before I noticed the spoon and that I didn't want to drink a beer with a spoon inside it. If she suspected I was a foreigner when she first saw me, then she confirmed her suspicions on hearing my accent and botched declinations. My memory of the incident ends there. I can't remember any longer whether I got my money back or got a new beer or got nothing. If I got a new beer, if I continued to sit there drinking it slowly, nursing it and enjoying her fuming, then I sure as hell hope I asked for an opener to crack off the cap myself!

On those winter walks in 1992, I normally went by myself. However, on one occasion the boy across the street came with me. He was Marko's grandson, who lived in the big new house Marko had constructed recently. The boy was the son of Marko's daughter, Zdenka, she being one of the two sisters who'd played with me back in 1969 and from whom I learned my first Croatian. He started showing up every day while we were visiting. I think he might have been drawn to me because I paid attention to him, talked about sports, and played soccer with him in the field outside the front door where I myself used to play in 1977. He seemed lonely. He was a biggish kid of about eleven, with ruddy healthy cheeks and big feet and hands, which for sure he inherited from his father, a Muslim from Bosnia whom no one seemed to talk about. He had lost most of his right foot when he stepped on a mine, though some people say he shot himself. The boy's father was gone a lot of the time for work, so maybe I was replacing the dad at some level. I don't know.

This I do remember very clearly. We were all watching the news one late morning, and the boy was there too. A report showed a Muslim paramilitary warlord (and former gangster) in Bosnia with the *nom de guerre* Juka (Jusuf Prazina). He and his militia were training in the snow, wearing black jumpsuits that had JUKA stitched on the front. The black-and-white TV gave this picture of tough insurgents the look of a World War II documentary and made them resemble the Partisans of that period. War often produces men like Tito or Juka who have constructed outsized and mythical personae out of modest and, in the case of Juka, criminal, pasts. Juka had grown up a troubled kid in an impoverished family, and by his own reckoning had spent more time behind bars than at home. In time, he built a debt-collecting enterprise in Sarajevo that led to him and his men brutalizing delinquent debtors by mangling their fingers or disfiguring their faces. When the war started, his gang of 300 became useful to the poorly armed defence forces of Sarajevo, and his pre-war criminality was overlooked by the Muslim-controlled government, so that he was named head of the Bosnian army's special forces. With his distinctive equine and lantern-jawed face, he became a noticeable figure; he was a hero to Sarajevans, and a patriotic Robin Hood to the foreign press. But his ongoing criminal activity, including privately beneficial collaborations with Republika Srpska officials, cocaine addiction, petulant narcissism, and ambition to climb the ranks of the Bosnian military led to a call for his arrest. Juka retreated to Mt. Igman, where he continued his criminal ways and where he joined the Croatian forces to fight the Bosnian army. Labelled a traitor by some, and with only two hundred of his most loyal men on Mt. Igman with him, he saw the writing on the wall, retreated to the Dalmatian coast, and eventually to Belgium, where he was discovered in a ditch by two Romanian hikers in 1993, dead of "lead poisoning" as a report in *Vreme* put it—two bullets in the head.

The footage of Juka we saw in Christmas 1992 appeared to have been from his time on Mt. Igman during his rapprochement with Bosnian-Croatian forces. That was why Croatian TV was showing a documentary about him. Miško, who had taken a break from his driving instructor work, and was watching the broadcast with us, wasn't impressed by the heroic persona of Juka. He thought Juka was an opportunist who was temporarily useful to the Croatian cause, which at that time was unification of Croatian parts of Bosnia-Herzegovina with Croatia proper. Miško had no sympathy for Juka's Muslim soldiers. When the Serbs attacked Vukovar, the Muslims in general hadn't take a stand against that aggression, he pointed out. "But now that the Serbs are raping their women," he said, "aahhh, now they run to us for help. Well, to hell with them."

The boy's reaction to the story about Juka was different. He smashed his fist on the table and screamed, "We have to explode the Serbs!" His face turned red, and he looked wildly around at us. Mila told him, "Hush, you don't know what you're talking about." She went to the cabinet and took out a package of *Napolitanke* wafers and put them in front of him. "Have one," she said. I remember pondering the possible conditions and influence at the boy's home that might have produced this reaction. If, indeed, anything or anyone influenced him.

The documentary about Juka was followed by a report about the U.N. presence in Bosnia. There were images of newly arrived peacekeepers carrying supplies into a building. A shell landed somewhere nearby, causing them to duck their heads and scurry into the building. Everyone in the kitchen laughed. Štefek said, "So this is who they're sending. First they sanction weapons so we can't defend ourselves, then they send cowards like this to protect us."

The next piece showed a crew from Britain's Sky News visiting a Serb unit in the hills above Sarajevo. They were drinking šljivovica and singing patriotic songs. When they noticed the cameras, they waved their guns menacingly and the journalists fled. Later, the journalists visited a friendlier group of Serbs who invited them to sit and chat. "We are tired of this war, this killing," one of them said. "We want to go home to our families. We have nothing against the Croats or Muslims. We only want to protect our people."

"These Serbs are okay," Miško said. "But even they talk about protecting their people. They see pictures on television, and they think we are all butchers. *Ustaša* butchers."

So, these were the sorts of conversations we had in Srebrnjak and elsewhere during this trip. We were on holiday, true, but disturbing stories began to reach me even here on the periphery of the war. Soon after arriving, I found out that even where there was no war there were war victims. Guns had flooded the black market, so accidental deaths and killings and suicides had spiked. There was Slavko Jakopač's son, Ivek, "The Moth," who was shot in the chest at a drunken party. The boy's aunt, his mother's sister, Milena whom I'd played with back in 1969, bought the pistol she carried in her purse for two months before apparently shooting herself late one evening at her boyfriend's apartment.

The worst case I heard of took place the next year. Tea's friend, Natalija, the black-haired girl who accompanied her on those walks in 1988 and whom I met on the road once, was murdered by her boyfriend, a young man without much going for him who had moved into the house with her and her parents. This choice of hers, the direction her whole life had gone, might have been some sort of psychologically complicated reaction to and rebellion against her upbringing. Her father was very proper and strict. As the story goes, her father laid down a hard law with her, tried to control her, forbade her certain things. But he was an honourable man too, they say, an ethnic Serb who had experienced persecution when the war started. With his daughter, it seemed that his strictness had had the exact opposite effect on her. Natalija rebelled and gravitated to the sex trade and had been working in a massage parlour. The father's decision to allow the boyfriend into his house turned out to be a fateful one, for the boyfriend strangled Natalija in the yard after she refused to quit her job. He then crept into the bedroom of the parents and hacked them to death with an axe. He hesitated, though, as he stood above the baby in the crib. He was unsure about killing her too, and just stood there for a moment. Without parents or grandparents, he thought, she would be without family and would end up in institutions, and that would be no life. It was mercy, he decided, that forced his hand. He took a knife and stabbed her through the chest. The blade went right through her into the mattress. But she didn't make a sound, he said at his trial.

Our vacation in Christmas 1992 occurred during a very dark period in Croatia's history, and I felt the reverberations in Srebrnjak during our visit. I felt ready to go back to my life at grad school, and I can say it is the only time I was happy to be leaving Srebrnjak.

But before I left, I took one last walk down the road to Brezje. I wanted to see the young woman I'd met in 1988, the one with whom I'd gone on that walk to Marija Magdalena. I knew she lived in the little wooden house on the road. But that was all I knew. Four and a half years had gone by. I wasn't sure she would even be there anymore. When I got a closer look at the house, it struck me as the worst one in the entire area, worst in the sense of poorest or most impoverished. It was a mainly wooden structure in the style of the oldest two-room peasant houses like the one my father was born in, with a meandering brick addition on the front. I didn't know it then, but the house where the murder took place was right next door. There was also a sloppily built barn made of wood and sheet metal that was three times the size of the house. I opened the gate, walked across the muddy yard to the front door and knocked. No one answered at first, so I knocked again. There was no car in the yard. Finally, the door swung open, forcing me to step back out of its way. The same curly blonde woman with green eyes faced me. I recognized her right off, but I wasn't sure she knew me. Even after I told her who I was I wasn't sure she remembered me. Her face expressed vacant disinterest. She seemed to look right through my body. What conversation we had I don't remember, but I know our conversation lasted only a minute or two and then ended, and that she never moved from the half open door and didn't invite me inside.

The Woman from Brezje + Pag

In 1991, my maternal grandmother, Oma, died of a second stroke. Alone of all my family, I happened to be in Edmonton at the time and visited her in the Misericordia Hospital every day after she'd been admitted, though I wasn't by her side at the final moment, having stepped out for a break from my vigil. Her death was a shock to me, even if it was anticipated, because she was the first person in my immediate family to die.

I returned to Fredericton, where I was working on my doctorate at the University of New Brunswick. In the months after Oma's death, I phoned my grandfather, Georg Panzer, regularly to keep up his spirits, and to give him someone to talk to. I called him around 5:00 in the evening his time, and invariably he was getting himself ready for bed. There was nothing left for him to do, and he was going to bed. By the time he woke up, it was midnight, so he had the rest of the night to contend with. His own Gethsemane. The man who had been imprisoned in a French prisoner-of-war war camp between 1943 and 1948, who had never spoken to me about it except once, on the very front steps of the house where I'd read *The Lord of the Rings* as a kid, told me almost nothing about the war except that he and the other prisoners were fed raw potato peels in the first months, which caused their bodies to bloat and which made them sick, who spent much of his Edmonton life finding refuge in his back yard and working in his garden, smoking cigarettes and nursing a warming beer, warding off his wife's regular censure of his character because of his supposed drinking problem and other shortcomings, the same man found it too much to live after her death. He lasted three months.

In 1993, Strina Slava followed my grandparents. During this period, then, three people who had known me as a boy died. Whatever memories they had of me were also gone. In a sense, a part of me was gone too. Until that moment, naively, I'd been oblivious to this reality about my aging that everyone eventually comes to know: that people's memories of you as a child die, that you become separated from a part of you that is unknown and unrecoverable. Maybe this is what Oma understood when she was impelled to tell me all those stories of her childhood.

But these feelings of mine passed. When I returned to Croatia again, things were looking good. I'd finished my doctorate, gotten my first teaching contract and earned the money to pay for my flight for the first time. By my sister's prompting I ignored my mother's nose-to-the-grindstone advice to carry on working out west where Joe lived after the end of my contract in Newfoundland and decided instead to enjoy the money I'd earned.

My decision had some important consequences. Yet again, I decided to visit the woman who hadn't given me the time of day the last time I was in Croatia. Why I went exactly, where my life would have gone had I not knocked on the door of the little house again, I don't know. But go I did, maybe not on the first day I was in Srebrnjak, nor the second, but soon after. I rode off on the same black bicycle I'd always ridden. Mila would shout at me, "*Kuda?*—Where to?" She would do this with increasing sarcasm as the days went by.

I parked outside the gate of the little peasant house and, somewhat nervously, knocked on the door again. This time the face that looked at me through the opened door recognized me right away. The eyes had more brightness and life. This time Tea said, "Come in! You can meet my daughter!" I was surprised. I had envisioned, I suppose, our story carrying on just as if no time had passed, our returning to our walk to Marija Magdalena and reliving it all over again. The contrail of that half-imagined storyline dissipated as I followed her into the small, creaky-floored kitchen and sat down on the u-shaped, padded bench that went around the table. A beautiful eighteen-month-old girl with large dark eyes and blonde curls just like Tea's clung to her mother when she came out of the bedroom, still sleepy after having woken. When she saw me, she gave me a similar, sullen, affectless "Who the fuck are you?" look perfected by her mother. And this without practice. Just came naturally to it!

FIGURE 9. Tea Hictaler in Brezje, 1996
FIGURE 10. Lora Hictaler in Brezje, ca. 1998

Tea explained her reaction the last time I came to visit as a gap in her memory caused by a bad and sometimes violent relationship from which she had been trying to escape.

I don't know if it was immediately then or days later that the situation of the two of them, mother and daughter living in a shack in a little village in Croatia, no husband or dad in the picture, opened up a door inside me that had been waiting for a while, had been waiting for the moment but had been closed. I was ready for something more serious, and this was more serious.

For the first time since 1988, Tea and I walked together in the hills while Tea's daughter Lora stayed at home under the care of Tea's foster mother, an illiterate and wildly vulgar woman who was fiercely loyal to the little girl and highly distrustful of me at the start. The hills above Brezje were unfamiliar to me. The whole area had started to change. I saw new weekend houses on the spine of the hills, new gated mansions of stone with security cameras and guard dogs that snarled at us as we passed; I saw upscale bungalows of brick like those in a north American suburbia, saw other houses built in the style of dark wooden peasant homes but modernized. On the opposite financial scale were many concrete slabs put there by owners who hadn't yet scraped together enough money for the rest of the structure, and in some cases never would. A new neighbourhood across the street from Tea's house was inhabited now by Croatians from Herzegovina who weren't exactly welcomed by the locals; they went to mass in Sveta Nedelja, where they sang the hymns in their own dialect, which irritated many long-time residents so much that they went to worship in Samobor instead. On this first walk with Tea I also saw new vineyards with concrete posts and green netting to protect the grapes from hail, as well as abandoned vineyards going to seed.

The newness of these vantage points combined with the newness of our rediscovery of each other. I can see Tea now.

A cataract of blonde curls, the swings of her curvy hips in jean cut-offs, the tight T-shirt, the legs. The melodic voice. She projected this fascinating image of a vaguely tragic *enfant sauvage* and Bambi Woods. Tea had been looking at me too. Once when we were enjoying the view, she turned to me and told me to take off my glasses. When I did, she said, "You have nice eyes. Actually, they're quite large. It's your lenses that make them smaller. They change your whole face. You should do something about that."

Farther on was an orchard of cherries. Tea, after casing the area, led me in by the hand. The cherries were very dark and ripe. When she picked them, she split open a few to check if there were worms. "These are fine," she told me. They tasted more richly sweet than the cherries I was used to. She faced me, cherry between her lips, tonguing the smooth skin, smiling. After she ate another cherry without opening it first, I asked her why and she answered, "This tree seems okay. But if not, what's an extra little meat going to do to you? Why so worried? Don't be a pubic louse." She told me her foster father, Marijan, who had died of cancer ten months before I came, used to steal into orchards and vineyards around here with an empty bag and then return with a filled one, managing somehow to avoid detection, or maybe not managing. Who knows, maybe that was one of the reasons the Ratkovići had a poor reputation. The only grapes he owned grew beside the house— red *Izabela*, or Concord, grapes. That reminded me, I told her, of my Croatian grandfather, the one who had died in 1943 fighting for the Domobrani. He too, they say, never used to come home empty-handed, bringing back not only fruit but wood, which was a more precious commodity during that scarcer time.

Farther up the lane along which we were walking was an unvisited weekend house, judging by the tall grass in the yard. Tea pointed out the spikes of the iron gate, said, "When I was a girl, I tried to climb this gate. My cousin Branko accidentally bumped me as I was trying to climb it. When I slipped, one of these spikes went into my leg, my shin. Here, look, you can see the hole still. The funny thing was there was no blood." She said she'd been a tomboy when she was younger and had beat up Branko all the time, one of the cousins she'd inherited when she was deposited among the Ratkovići.

In a glade, protected from the sight of the neighbours, as shafts of afternoon sun shone through the trees and white butterflies danced around us, we sat and talked. We revisited our brief history together, remembered our first meeting and our first walk to Marija Magdalena. She laughed and said I was a nerd, with my glasses and tucked-in shirt and *futbalerka* mullet. Coming closer, green eyes lit by the sun filtering through the leaves, she whispered, "I'm going to have to do something about that."

Later, we walked on for kilometres in the direction of Sveti Martin pod Okićem, a village with a ruined castle on a high peak among undulating blue hills to the south. Hours went by and the sun set. On our return we went through the village of Dol and ended up passing the house belonging once to Slavko Jakopač, who had died. In the dark I could make out the wooden table in the yard where he and I had sat and drunk wine nine years ago. Farther on was the house at the crossroads belonging to Jana and Dragec. I could see the windows upstairs of Vlado's and Željka's bedrooms.

As Tea and I neared the crossroads, a young man heard us talking and laughing and stepped out of his house. He was pointing a rifle at us. "What are you doing making this noise?" he demanded, the rifle waving up and down unsteadily. The streetlight cast a hollow glow and lit the gun dully. I am gun-shy, as in shy of a gun pointed at me in the dark by some possibly crazy guy with a temper who's had too much to drink. So I turned tail. Without looking away from the man, Tea grabbed my shirt and pulled me back. "Where are you going?"

She stood in front of the guy with the rifle pointed at her. The thought didn't come to me at the moment; I was just stuck in my tracks watching the scene unfold as though I weren't part of it. But I wonder now as I write whether some other imperative—a moral rectitude against cowering, a stubborn refusal to back down—played a part in her standing up to him too. "Listen," she said calmly, "We were just passing by and didn't mean any harm. Why don't you put the gun down and go back into to your house?"

"I heard a noise. You were making noise, laughing, and it is night," he said lamely, with less assurance.

She told him with the same measured voice and tone that we had a right to laugh and to walk on the street, no matter what time it was, and that we were sorry if we had caused a disturbance and we were moving on anyway and wouldn't it be best if he just took his gun and went inside? He stood there not saying anything, the gun waving a little back and forth.

At that point, an older man poked his head out the door and ordered his son into the house. The guy with the gun hesitated. "Watch yourself. You watch yourselves now, coming around here." Then he went inside. Tea told me as we walked back to Brezje that the guy's father was the butcher who had killed their cow so they could pay for the funeral of her adoptive father, Marijan.

I was relaxed again as we walked back to Brezje. This was the same road down which Tea and Natalija had met me years ago, the same road Željka and I had ridden on the way back from Zagreb. Tea and I passed in and out of pools of light from the streetlamps, past houses with open windows, white curtains visible in the dark. One man was snoring so loudly we heard him fifty metres away. I asked Tea whether this thing with the guy and the gun, her walking with some foreigner at night, was going to make her the object of gossip. "I don't care," she said, "we weren't doing anything wrong."

The days went by with more of these walks, sometimes just the two of us, sometimes with Lora in her stroller. I didn't know it then but it would be the last summer of staying in the house in Srebrnjak, the last summer I would ride that black bike, the last time I would hear Mila's sarcastic "Kuda, Tony?" as I drove down the Srebrnjak road and she'd spied me when she came out of the barn after milking the cows, though I never heard Štefek make any remark, because he was of the attitude that it was none of his business to meddle in another person's affairs.

But in that spring of 1996, I was still single and could still travel freely. The war was over by then and I was ready to embark on an ambitious walking trip down the Adriatic coast. That had been a main reason for my coming to Croatia, not to find love. And so there I was hitchhiking on the Magistrala Highway looking out at the white barren flank of Pag.

The sun was already high, its wicked light hurtful to the eyes, and the bright sea sparkled then, farther out, melted into the horizon. On my head was my khaki safari hat from Canadian Tire and on my back a canvas knapsack that sweated up my back and that I shut with a safety pin.

My first impression of Pag was shaped by my experience on another island, different from it in almost every way, but similar in the feeling it produced in me. The previous year I had arrived on the Rock of the North Atlantic, Newfoundland, on a teaching contract. My trip there, my stay through fall and winter, suggested the similarity, not difference between these two island rocks. On that first drive across Newfoundland, I remember how the Trans-Canada, or TCH, as was painted in faded white on the blacktop, took me at first past the Long Range Mountains. The tops of the mountains seemed sheared off and stunted pines grew up the sides almost to the summit. The morning sun, which shone from behind them, left their western face in a dark blue shade. They looked vast and ominous, and the overriding feeling they gave me was of a huge implacable force brooding over the puny human life that scurried back and forth on the road nearby. The country unfolding over the next couple hundred kilometres—the wide tundra-like spaces, boggy in the summer, open howling wastes in the winter, the anemic pines leaning to one side from the prevailing wind, the fast-moving black-water rivers bursting out of black forest—can be described as the sublime.

The sublime, Edmund Burke said, is often confused with the beautiful, but a beautiful landscape—pretty meadows, softly undulating hills, gentle valleys, exactly the sort of place that Srebrnjak is—seems safe and pliable to human will, whereas a sublime one does not. Nevertheless, despite our sense of weakness before the sublime, we search it out, find pleasure in it even, and consider it beautiful, in a generic sense. It might be that a sublime landscape is awesome and worthy of respect, that because it is more powerful than we are, it is worth worshipping, is divine. So not knowing it, on my first trip, I was viewing Newfoundland in these terms.

Similarly, my walk to Pag was fretted with dark worry. The island cast a haunting aura of fear and awe when I saw it up close for the first time. Not far off the coast, it is a low cream-white strip of jagged karst like the back and tail of a plated beast—massive, hostile, and empty. From the mainland the island looked to me even more barren than Rab, so that the usual word used to describe this side of Pag, a "moonscape," remains probably the best one.[8]

The feeling Pag projected intensified as I trudged along the highway. Few cars passed by, and I was alone. The only sounds were my own footsteps, the cicadas in the rocky fields and a soft mewing of sea gulls high on the left, against the backdrop of the Velebit Mountains unspooling grey-blue into the distance.

---

8 Predrag Matvejević in *Mediterranean*: "Dalmatia was thickly wooded at one time, but the Venetians' practical bent took care of that, and the Slavs' impractical bent has kept the trees from growing back" (36).

I've written about this experience before, but now, after all these years, I better understand my own situation in the wider context of the country itself. I was entering a new phase, just as Croatia itself was. It was a year after the end of the Yugoslav war, around ten months since Croatian forces had completed their *Oluja* ("Storm") offensive into the Krajina, reclaiming territory seized by the Serbs, so the whole region had the reputation of instability and danger. No one from the rest of the world was here. I was a solitary traveller at a special moment in Croatian history.

At first, I enjoyed the solitude. I didn't think of the people in Srebrnjak, nor of my recent experiences with Tea. All of that was behind me.

But soon the pleasures of solitude were driven off by the relentless heat of the sun. I crisscrossed the empty road, searching out shade from stone walls. The wind from the sea cooled me, but the ferry terminal for Pag was still fifteen kilometres distant. It would take me hours to get there. I knew I was overmatched.

FIGURE 11. View of the island of Pag from the bridge

The guy in the rusted white vw Rabbit who picked me up was a big black-haired army corporal with dense eyebrows, a hooked nose and a right thumb that looked like it had been melted off then glued back on. He said he was returning to his wife and kids after a three months' tour in the military. He lived in Zadar, fifty kilometres south of Pag, which could be reached more easily by continuing on the Magistrala. Still, he offered to take me to Pag, a detour for him, and even paid for my ferry ticket. I was suspicious. I wondered why he offered help to a stranger when he should have been keener on getting back home to his family. Nevertheless, I went with him.

On the boat he scared the hell out of me. "See this," he growled, pointing to a scar on his left arm. "Serb sniper almost got me. Lucky I moved at the last second." He glanced at the water then back at me. "I was carrying a howitzer, so I pointed it at the fucker and killed him." His face froze into a smile, and goosebumps sprang up on his arms. He waited, gauging my reaction. "Boom," he added.

I had nothing to say. A nervous thrill washed over me, but I pretended to be cool. Instead of facing his eyes, I looked at the island approaching. Like my mood in that moment, Pag seemed desolate: no trees, no shelter, no life. This side of Pag seemed a real rock, far more inhospitable than Newfoundland, so I had trouble imagining that there was anything worth seeing.

But soon my thoughts began to change. When we docked and drove off, we soon reached the summit of the island from where the land slopes down to the sea on the southern coast and evergreen maquis is sprinkled between the island's white rock. Olive trees scattered here and there were bent away from the sea like stooped old men. Stone walls lashed down the island like ropes securing cargo when the bura blows in the winter. A hot wind blasted through our open windows, carrying the same curry aroma I'd smelled on Rab. The perfumes of other herbs, more muted, wafted in as well.

The car sped along, and my worries left me as I watched the arid but beautiful landscape pass by. I was grateful for the ride, ashamed of my suspicions. I realize now, as I write, that my driver had known better than I did the difficulty of hitching a ride off the ferry. A long walk across Pag in the blistering heat had awaited me. He had been looking out for me.

Soon we made an ascent and cut through an opening at the top of the island, from where we could see the town of Pag far below simmering in the heat. I said goodbye to my driver, who wrote his name and address in Zadar on a piece of paper, and invited me to his place, any time, any time at all.

The town of Pag was built in the form of a grid with two wide streets meeting at right angles, dividing the town in four, at the centre of which was a spacious main square and a large fifteenth-century church. The flagstones on the main streets were wide and smoothly polished; the façades of the houses had been redone, shutters newly painted white and the wooden doors green and brown. Pag's linear design gave the town a clean open feeling unlike that of other medieval coastal towns with their warren-like streets.

I walked to the stone waterfront. Three or four cafés, bordered by squat palm trees, waited for the summer crowd. A few men smoked over a beer or coffee. At dock was a sailing vessel, its sails brailled up on the masts. It was the same one I would see in later years, always in the same spot. The heat had slowed down the day, and a thick languid breeze ruffled the flags on the ship. The water gurgled sleepily against its brown flanks. In the distance was a big beach curving in an arc, and on the hills a few houses scattered along the lower slopes.

I bought half a loaf of bread, a smoked sausage, and some slices of *paški sir*, Pag's hard, sharp ewe's cheese. From my spot in the shade I ate and looked out at the barren white section of the island across the bay, darkened by shadows from the clouds, as a few white boats bobbed in the harbour. Behind me, a street led to the centre of the old town. Few people walked along the dock and there were no tourists at all.

Having finished lunch, I explored the wide, clean-swept streets of the town. The simple, square buildings were two storeys high, painted soft pastel colours, beige, lime and yellow. My footsteps echoed down the long narrow spaces. On the main street a man was talking with an old woman dressed in black and sitting on her stool. Farther down, well-spaced out from each other, were other old women, one dozing, another sewing intricate pieces of *čipka*, her finished lacework displayed like big snowflakes in the window of her house. Many of these snowy windows were on show throughout town.

I stopped to watch the woman sew. Her hands moved with practised precision, her head bent over a section of lace on a green pillow backing. Her blouse was light blue, metal hair-pins kept her bun in place, and she wore a blue skirt draped to the ground.

"Very nice," I said after a while. "How much?"

She pointed up at the window, not looking at me. "This one is 100 *kuna*, this one 150." About 25 to 40 dollars for around eight square inches.

"Do you work every day?"

"Not every day."

"Today you're outside."

"Yes, there's a breeze and the light is good."

I wondered why she was facing the window rather than the street. Looking to my right I saw another woman a few doors down seemingly asleep.

"She's not sewing čipka," I said.

Without looking up, she answered "Never has."

I assumed the neighbour was a friend of hers, but when I mentioned something to that effect the woman still sewing answered, "We don't talk much. I don't think we've spoken in the last month." Her head was down as she continued to work so I said goodbye and walked on.

Not long after speaking to the old lace-maker, I had another encounter with a woman, this time without conversation.

Having explored the town by then, the sun shining wickedly, I decided to go for a swim to cool off. The main beach in Pag town is a long arc of stone shingles at the head of the bay. Besides a wooden skiff that had been pulled onto shore, the beach was empty. The sea was a motionless slab of light jade. Against my hot skin the water felt cool as I front-crawled out to sea.

When I returned and stood up in waist-deep water, recovering, I noticed I was no longer alone on the beach. A young woman with a baby in a stroller had parked herself a few steps from my towel. She had dark hair and wore a short sleeveless dress of blue and white. Two ideas went through my mind: the first was that she had chosen a spot so close to mine on a vast, empty beach. The second idea was a directive to myself that I should get out of the water and move my things. A person with no sense of appropriate social distancing ought to be taught a lesson. What was she thinking, anyway? But I didn't move my things, didn't do anything, just stood there in the water looking out to sea and back to the beach.

FIGURE 12. Woman in Pag sewing lace, 1996

The woman checked on her baby and, when she found everything in order, the baby sleeping, I guess, she began to undress. She kicked off her sandals, slipped out of her dress, and then removed her bikini top as well. In the second it took for me to turn away, I saw that her breasts were paler than the rest of her.

She walked into the water just a few metres from me, splashed herself, her arms and her shoulders, and then her breasts. She did it in a way that reminded me of elderly women preparing themselves for a dip. Except she wasn't elderly. I pretended to concentrate on the white clouds above the bone-coloured limestone hills to the north. My eyes panned in the other direction, to the hills to the south, but at the same time, without being too obvious about it, back to the woman's shapely and ample breasts.

She didn't notice. Didn't seem to notice me at all. Not once did she look in my direction or say anything out loud, not even an innocuous "Nice day" or "The water is warm"—nothing. I seemed no more consequential to her than the wooden skiff dragged onto the beach. I didn't talk to her either. I was inside the moment, mute and indecisive. A parallel possibility, a woman with a child, had appeared to me like some temptation or test from God. What would have happened had I started a conversation? Where would this all have gone? Was I going to miss out if I did nothing? I would never find out. I don't even know whether these questions entered my mind at the time. She slipped under the water finally and swam a few strokes and then returned to the baby. I swam a little longer before going back to my towel and drying off. The baby woke up and the woman began to fuss over it. She had become a mom again. I lay there for a few more minutes before I stuffed my things into my pack and went back to town.

And so the scene ended and would have died forever were it not for the act of writing that brought it back to my memory. Various interpretations of who this woman was and what was going on swim through my mind now. As I write I think it possible she came to the beach every day and I was the one intruding on *her* familiar spot. I was nobody to her and she had a husband working back in Zagreb, or somewhere. Or maybe there was no husband, no anybody; maybe he had died in the war (there were many widows at that time). In that case, I *was* a somebody. She was another single mom like Tea and was interested in a young guy alone on a beach who looked like a foreigner, a rich foreigner (except, of course, there was that old canvas backpack and wrinkly safari hat that seemed to torpedo that possibility). She had seen *me* and had come to the beach on purpose. Or maybe she had none of those intentions; perhaps she had just imagined herself spending an afternoon with someone who wasn't from around here and looked like he was moving on. . . .

I was moving on, walking down a baking slab of concrete on the way to Povljana, a village by the sea. The highway south of Pag town cut through a wide valley bordered by white hills. A yellow sign pointing me to the right read "Povljana 7 km." The narrow, paved road brought me into a flat stone-pocked land, with fields of sparse yellow grass stretching all the way to the sea, marked off by the same hip-high rock walls that held down the whole island and divided the land into big pastures. Gaunt sheep huddled near the road in the narrow shade of a wall, holding out against the sun as it crossed the scoured blue sky. On other trips here, I used to see sheep walking in formation along Pag's narrow roads, their wool the same cream colour as the stones, always a single black back in the herd. Today I noticed a shepherd's hut of rough blocks and small rectangular windows in an empty field and then a sign that Povljana was not too far, a marshy inlet to my right and a small fishing boat on the land, half busted, bleached by the sun.

It was peaceful. As I walked through this wide open space, I felt detached from things, from the world of people I'd left

behind in Pag town, even from my own self—a feeling of separation from everything that was me that I would have now and again on my solitary travels. The sparse world of Pag, the white bony landscape in which the only living things I saw were lizards scurrying off their sunning spots and black and grey snakes whipping their tails at me when I approached, seemed to erase my own identity into nothing.

The feeling continued for a while as I came to the village in the quiet afternoon and made my way down the main street past the post office towards the sea. I had drifted in there like a ghost. No one had seen me. No one was in sight, not a soul moving, no sound of children playing or people talking to break the silence. Doors were open, but no one going in or out. Fruit, vegetables, and weigh scales sat on the cement and rock walls that lined the street, but there was nobody to buy from. In the courtyards shaded by grapes or fig trees, the tables sat empty. Finally, through branches of a tree, I saw a foot on a hammock, then the body of an old guy having a nap.

FIGURE 13. Sheep on the island of Pag

But I saw no one else. The heat was stifling. Everything seemed to have slowed down and even the wind that gently swayed the trees felt thick and sluggish. Farther on, where the sea became visible, I saw a boat frozen near the horizon, and flags on the skiffs at dock furling and unfurling slowly. From the dock I saw a small bay and a peninsula—a long, rocky finger dusted by grass and thatched with pines. Rock walls zigzagged over the top and down the other side. Just above the main beach stood a small stone chapel, and a cemetery grown over with tall grass, its crosses leaning left and right.

The boats bobbing up and down made the water gurgle sleepily, and I dropped my pack and lay on the dock. I was tired, hungry too. It seemed that I, like the rest of Povljana, was succumbing to the *fjaka*.

The fjaka is often associated in Croatia with the people farther south in Dalmatia, though that doesn't necessarily have to be the case. Jakša Fiamengo has presented it like this: "If we were to attribute all our moods to the seasons, the fjaka, as a specific state of mind and body, could be said to be a conspicuous product of the summer, the result of its sweltering heat, and a general dissolution of body and spirit in the baleful high temperatures of the day, when we just don't feel like doing anything. But this doesn't mean that we don't succumb to the fjaka in other seasons as well—because it is primarily a state," as he further explains, "which is beyond control and thus defies set definitions and names: it cannot be categorized either as a layabout idleness or as relaxed respite from everyday life, or as a phlegmatic state, or as leisure time, chronic listlessness, or the mere slowing down of life functions. Actually it is, and at the same time it is not, a mixture of all of the above." [9]

---

[9] Jakša Fiamengo, "The Fjaka, As a Specific State of Mind and Body," *Crown Croatia World Network.* http://www.croatia.org/crown/articles/9842/1/Fjaka---Between-Times.html.

As I lay on the dock, in a fjaka like the rest of Povljana, I understood its hypnotizing mood. The pine forest sighed coded messages to the seagulls whirling around the treetops. Motionless, the boat on the horizon seemed forever delayed on its journey home. I lingered for a while, then picked up my pack and walked back up the road.

In the spirit of the fjaka, Povljana too is relaxed in its spatial design and its daily human life. There is no centre, and the streets wander to the country or sea in no rush to take you there. On these casual thoroughfares, villagers go slowly about their business. I saw shepherds herding their flocks through the village, bells clanging, and farmers driving past on one-man tractors, handlebars extended from the engine like those on a Harley, and old ladies in black roosting after mass outside the main church, and tall, darkly-handsome Casanovas with cropped hair and flip-flops and cigarettes in hand striding into a café, from which the loud voices of men inside greeted them, and vans dropping off fish at the store early in the morning, some of which ended up for sale on walls beside the wine and vegetables.

The way to the main beach was a footpath through parcels of farmers' fields and gardens where bees droned and finches swooped from tree to tree. Lined with villas, the road became a short gravel stretch curving beside a field, a rock wall and Sveti Nikola chapel. The walkway to the chapel was made of stone slabs that looked like sarcophagi carved with unreadable inscriptions. A slit of a window in the western side, sun shining through, gave me a view of the rounded interior: a small altar, a wooden crucifix, a rickety dais with a half-melted candle, three wooden benches. A swallow's nest was tucked into one corner and cobwebs hung everywhere else. I turned from the door and took in the view of the sea, the fields, the peninsula to the left. A new section of Povljana had begun to grow across the bay to the right. A modern world encroaching.

A few years later there would be a bar near the chapel, built on a concrete slab, which sold drinks and ice cream to beachgoers and had loud music blaring, whose owner wanted to make a buck and didn't care that his bar ruined the scene.

But the rest of old Povljana wasn't changing. The village was positioned by the sea, would always rely on it. Povljana always looked inland too, and its villagers always depended on its gardens and fields. An amphibious place, a village of the sea and of the land, Povljana was a bit of Srebrnjak and a bit of the regular coast combined.

When summer ended and Povljana emptied and life slowed down even more, on quiet days through the fall and winter, the locals sat for long hours in cafés talking politics or playing cards or drinking or watching soccer. I thought of arguments that might flare up and then die out after a few hours, or longer—who knows how long these things last in villages like this. I wondered if Predrag Matvejević was right when he wrote about arguments among men of the sea, whether his comments were even applicable to amphibious Povljana, its men not all men of the sea. "True fisherman . . . lose their temper and quarrel (over bad weather, a bad catch, or bad workers), but do not fight like, say, dockers, or common peasants. When arguments break out among them (as they do over to and from which side to cast the net or when and how to haul it in), they never reach the intensity of arguments over who owns what land. The sea is easier to divide than the land because it is harder to own." [10]

On those winter days, boredom settled on the village as the north wind kept people inside and the grey waves slammed against the harbour walls. It was a very different world, the winter world of Povljana, of the Adriatic, a little dismal and sombre, one I never got to know and could never associate with my experiences in the hot summer on the islands.

10 Predrag Matvejević, *Mediterranean: A Cultural Landscape*, trans. Michael Henry Heim (Berkeley: University of California Press, 1999), 34.

Transitions, Departures

If I never got to know the winter in the Adriatic, I certainly came to know it in the north. When I returned to Croatia again, it was Christmas 1996. This time I stayed with Tea in her mother's shack in Brezje. With that decision I set in motion the next significant stage of my life, changed the relationship with the people I had known all these years, and shucked my youthful, single self. Nothing was going to stop me. Yet every decision has consequences.

I exacerbated things by not visiting Srebrnjak immediately on my arrival. When I did go, I went on my own, and Mila let me have it, "You've been here two days, two days, and you didn't visit!" The phone rang and when Mila answered, she said, "Tony is here! And guess what? He's not staying with me. No! Not here. In Brezje! With the Ratkovići!"

Joe, too, gave me an earful over the phone. He ordered me to visit anyone of consequence in our extended family. It didn't matter to him that I had no way of getting around other than by foot or bus. I admit following through obsequiously, even going so far as asking Tea to wait outside Miško's house in Samobor while I said hello to him, his wife, and their

children because I suspected their disapproval of my choice, and couldn't count on them treating Tea properly, or even letting us in. Or that's what the daughter had slyly hinted at. I remembered Strina Slava closing the door on Tea in 1988.

When I left the house, Tea tore into me. "What a coward you are! How can you do this to me? I'm so ashamed. Forced to stand out here like a dog. You have got to be enough of a man to let everyone know who I am to you. Pathetic!"

Despite these problems, that Christmas stands out for me as a special one, a glorious pause during which I lived each day without anxiety about what lay ahead, the reading I had to do, the syllabuses I had to prepare, or anything else about the future. I played with Lora in the little bedroom, tossing her into the air and catching her giggling on the bed. Through the cold, smoke-filled air, Tea and I walked into the hills every day. We spray-painted pinecones golden to decorate our Christmas tree. When snow fell heavily for days, we walked through a wonderland along the same lanes and through the same orchards that we had the previous summer. When it warmed and then rained and then froze, the pendent branches of the trees turned to glass, so that the country was made of crystal that gleamed under moonlight. And then we had each other at night, our quiet conversations, the intense electrodermal contact of our bodies, as Lora slept in the crib and the old woman moved around the kitchen, not always quietly, not trying to be quiet, even hacking up rattling gobs of phlegm and spitting them noisily into the wood stove, which was for us just an annoyance far on the edge of our awareness or caring.

The tension and bad feeling between myself and my Croatian family passed, leaving me at the end with a tempered, more realistic attitude about these people, the people I'd known since boyhood, a reconcilement with who they were, the generation and culture to which they belonged.

During this period, I got to know others in the area that I might not have otherwise. One of these was Marko, Štefek's brother. He saw Tea and me walking down the road in Srebrnjak and invited us into his house. He lived there with his wife, his daughter, who was one of the two girls whom I played with in 1969, his grandson, the boy I got to know in the winter of 1992 who had smashed his fist on the table in anger at the Serbs, and the boy's father, who wasn't there when we visited. I will never know what made Marko invite us in. Maybe it was just coincidental hospitality. Maybe he'd gotten wind of my new situation and wanted to be friendly. His wife Mima brought us coffee and some cookies, and we sat there for an hour talking about I know not what. It felt good for a while to know that not everyone was against Tea and me. Marko and Mima had gone through their own hell four years earlier with the death of their other daughter, but here they were supporting us, even if they didn't know it.

Mima was a simple, willowy woman with teeth missing, whom Mila used to mock because she milked her cows at midnight. Joe said he talked to Mima a few years later upon his departure for Canada, saw her as she was stepping out of the house and complaining to him of a headache and nausea that she blamed on eating a pear that had been sitting outside too long. As it turned out, she wasn't being honest about what had happened to her. When he arrived back home, he heard that Mima had died from her headache, from the trauma of a blow, and was to be buried that coming Saturday.

Marko lived on a few years. Then I got wind of a story about him. He had knocked on Mila's door one night, well after midnight, asking to stay there, having escaped through a window of his own house. The door had been locked against him. The next day he went home, then, a few weeks later, moved into an institution for the elderly. Eventually he returned to his house, but soon after became sick and was found in the pigsty, cold and soiled and no longer coherent. His daughter called the ambulance, but he died the next day or day after. Details were sketchy, but Mila had a pretty clear idea of who was responsible for what happened to Marko. No one I called from Canada about the situation wanted anything to do with it. This cold consensus, benign neglect, or perhaps fear, angered me about the people there. I had expected moral outrage and action. Marko was family, after all. But, instead, I got nowhere.

During this period, Tea and I also socialized with other members of my Croatian family whom I'd hadn't seen much over the years. These included Mila's sister Draga and her husband Ivek. They had moved out of their house in Samobor to live in their cottage in Srebrnjak, partly to make room for their son, his wife and two children. The son was the guy who had played guitar at the pig roast on our last family trip. Mila said he had failed to pay the house's power bill, so the power had been cut off. Her eager gossip about Draga's situation might have prompted Draga to invite us over, who knows? We visited them several times over the next few years, sitting on their small terrace by their grove of plum trees. Ivek smoked one cigarette after another, drank gemišt, and talked politics in that gravelly, dysphonic voice of his, acerbically making fun of my accent and expressions. Draga talked with Tea, brought out cakes she had baked and asked us about our plans, where we were going to live and so on. I have pleasant memories of these evenings; they were a sort of affirmation of my decision, and of my sense that not everyone was overly invested in negative judgement and snobbish moralizing.

Then there was the Rudolf family in Brezje whose daughters were friends of Tea's and whose old man, "Charlie," had taught my father in the 1950s at the school in Sveta Nedelja.

That Christmas of 1996 was the first of many late-night drink fests over the years with Neven, the husband of one of the daughters, a former professional water polo player in the Croatian first division and geological engineer. Neven was a tall, handsome man with a charming smile whose nationalism and social conservatism were typical of Croatian sportsmen of his generation, and whose brash loudness and ravings and gesticulations got more and more entertaining as the drinking went deeper into the evenings and early mornings, or more stupid if you came at it from the point of view of his wife (not unlike my own ravings after too much brandy and my soppy crocodile tears on one occasion when my son tried to get me into the car and I fell onto the concrete and he drove off without me). Neven would yell, "CRO-A-A-T-I-A-A-A" or say, "Tony, in dees moment of speaking, I tfink you need gemišt. Here, give glass." His English was worse than my Croatian, but somehow we managed to understand each other well. The sober other side of him was very loyal to family but also darker and more sensitive. After his company went under so that he was forced to work for others, he turned to gardening and to religion, going faithfully to mass every Sunday with his brother-in-law, Ivica, whose family used to own the mill across from Tea's place, and who himself had gone through the hell of war, not speaking for months after his return home.

When Tea and I married in the summer of 1997, no one from my Croatian family attended other than Vlado (as best man), his son, Mislav, and Miško's son, Mario. Neither my father nor mother were there nor my sister, who couldn't afford to come. Miško sent a canister of his wine and Mila a single chicken. The next day Miško showed up asking for the empties back and any remaining wine. Despite these slights the day went off without a hitch and remains a nice memory. I took the bus in the morning to buy wine and brandy, and Tea's mother, Draga, who had only recently mistrusted me and made her feelings known by hawking gobs of spit into that stove every evening, came around to the idea of Tea and me together and covered the cost of the food, preparing it all with some friends and calling me affectionately "Tono" now, informing me that her pension from her employment at a pharmaceutical company had left her precariously short every month, giving me a sidelong look every time she told me so, and then at the wedding crying into a handkerchief when Tea, the only daughter she had ever known, dressed beautifully in a white dress with small white and yellow roses in her hair, her breasts all perfume, said yes, I will, yes. The Ratkovići daughters set the tables, arranged the cold cuts, and helped otherwise, even though they hardly knew me. The little time I had spent with that family was playing soccer with the brothers in the abandoned mill on summer evenings (not one of the brothers showed up). Yet with Tea's close friends from Brezje and Zagreb, and neighbours who'd known her for her entire life there, such as friendly, round-bellied, gregarious Pepo with all his ideas for striking it rich, like the plan for a travelling door-to-door massage business that never panned out and whose additions to his house looked as though they just might collapse from the next stiff breeze, the wedding was a friendly, casual not soigné affair, where everyone went away feeling good. Even if it wasn't a "real wedding," as Mila informed me.

After Tea and Lora emigrated, we returned five times in the next nine years. Our son, Lucas, was born on 23 April 2000 (Shakespeare's birthday and Easter Sunday). Somehow, I shoe-horned myself into a permanent post in academia. When I returned to Croatia in 2006, I went alone, having enough funds that year to cover my research on my book about Bosnia.

I drove to Srebrnjak and spent an afternoon there. Things had gone back to normal by then, and Mila had gotten used to the idea of Tea and me as a couple. One thing that broke the ice was the smoked sausages she'd offered us during our visit in 1998. The sausages had been boiled to an inch of their lives so that you needed a strong set of teeth to chew them, and when Tea had tried to stick a fork into hers, the fork deflected off the sausage and the sausage leapt off the plate and onto the floor. It lay there forlornly for a second. There was a momentary, awkward pause, then Mila laughed, and we all laughed. She threw the sausage into the pig pail and gave Tea another. So that sausage, anyway, set in motion a sort of normalcy from then on.

There was nothing memorable about my visit to the house in Srebrnjak in 2006, nor can I recall what we talked about. But there was this. Štefek said he wanted to show me something outside. It was the first and only time he had ever done so. I followed him under the walnut tree by the well and to a wide swath of land behind his barn that stretched 300 metres from the road all the way to the top of the hill. Štefek pointed to a path of destruction in the soil, the earth torn up and piled all around. "Atomska bomba," he said, with a laugh. It was a good description. I knew right away what he was showing me. In the midst of the torn earth I could see the footings of the house Joe was starting to build. He had shown me the blueprints the year before. Six bedrooms, five bathrooms, terraces on front and back. The house would be built on the same piece of land where he had been born, where the little peasant farmhouse had stood in which he and the others had lived all those years ago. The new place was going to be very different. The significance of this new house built on the land where the old one had stood, where my father had been born, wasn't lost on me, and I'm sure Štefek understood it as well. But he was a practical man, so it didn't surprise me when he said, "Velika, pre velika—Big, too big." He was right, the house was too big. There were all kinds of reasons against it being that big. But I could also see how it couldn't be anything other than what it was.

FIGURE 15. Štefek in the kitchen in Srebrnjak, ca. 2005

We walked back to the house and we said our goodbyes. I was leaving for Canada in a few days. I can see Štefek now as we shake hands. He is smiling, the last of the afternoon sun shows his face clearly to me. The sharp eyes, hooked nose, the brown cap. It was the last time I saw him alive. He died in January 2008, having come downstairs before Mila to start the fire, as he did every morning. Sitting on the wood box, where Strina Slava used to sit, he was tying his boots when he just slumped to the ground. The thud was loud enough to startle Mila upstairs. The moment she saw him sprawled on the floor, a shooting pain stabbed her eye and she lost sight in it forever.

Srebrnjak Mansion
✝ Cres ✝ Vis

Seven years went by before I returned. During that time, Joe completed his house. It rose from the atomic bomb site to its grand final form of granite, slate, and marble. At a time when all the working peasants other than Tomo had died out and only one cow remained and weekend houses had sprung up throughout the valley, a modern world encroaching, his modern house was a crazy and beautiful anomaly.

I flew into Frankfurt then drove south through Bavaria. The next day I passed through the bright green valleys and soaring cloud-ripping peaks of the Austrian Alps, so that my arrival in Srebrnjak, into a small valley between low hills, low compared to the mountains, made me realize how unlike the sublime it was.

I noticed some changes. The weathered wooden crucifix had been replaced by one made of concrete and plastic, and the road was paved all the way up the valley, widening to two lanes near Joe's place. There were curbs now. Where once there had been a ditch along the side of the road in which ducks swam, now there were underground pipes bringing water efficiently from Samobor.

I arrived at the gate. I stopped the car, let the engine idle and looked up at the house. It seemed to have taken over the land around it. I thought of Joe's assiduous care with the planning and construction, like his purchasing every piece of stone from China rather than from the stone yard in Sveta Nedelja three kilometres away (because, he claimed, it was cheaper); I remembered all the delays in getting building approvals, the shiftlessness of hired workers when he was in Vancouver earning the money for the place, the loss of the first footings because of an earth slide, and the near catastrophe of bankruptcy and having to build himself back up. To my eye, sure, there were also questionable decisions like a driveway made entirely of grey granite bricks that had started to sink in places and through which weeds grew. There was the craziness of the size. But the overall effect, when I took everything into account, was impressive. It was a symbol for his entire life. The completion of a full circle.

I drove up the driveway and parked in front of the garage and greeted Joe when he came out.

"What took you so long," he asked. "Did you get lost?"

"What do you mean? I did 130 the whole time," I said.

"Which direction did you go?"

"Villach direction."

"That explains it, that road is longer."

"Yeah, but the views are great. It's not how fast you come, but the experience. Don't you know that? Anyway, I'm here now."

I looked him over. Eight years had gone by since I'd last seen him. He was barefoot, shirtless and wore khaki shorts and a brown leather belt I'd given him ten years ago. Around his neck was a fat gold chain from a former girlfriend. His arms looked skinnier. The leathery hide of his super-tanned skin hung looser.

"You should do some push-ups," I told him.

"I do push-ups every day."

"You do?"

"Every day.... When I dig with the shovel," he cackled.

"Not the same."

"Oh, you're going to see, you'll see. There's some work I have waiting for you, plenty, just for you sonny boy!"

"Just the reason I came."

His wife, Denise, came out, a Vancouverite of Slovenian background with high cheekbones and a bobbed haircut like the women of the 1920s. She was a former corporate secretary, highly organized, and was responsible for choosing the furniture

FIGURE 16. Joe Fabijančić on his back terrace, 2013.

in the house, much of which came from Bali—the incredible wooden tables with elaborate carvings of rice farmers ploughing with cattle and other scenes, all encased by glass, the other furniture like the massive armoires of solid wood, the corners decorated with carved pheasants, ears of wheat, cobs of corn.

After we'd eaten, my father gave me a tour of the house. I think he wanted to see it through my eyes. The physical house, I mean. Its position on the land, whether purposeful or accidental, and the deeper experiential feelings that that produced in me over time were something else altogether. We started out front, where a winding staircase of granite with a wrought-iron railing led to the second level, a stair we never used. On this second level, the front door of Balinese teak that weighed 200 kilos and had to be brought in by crane, was also never used. On either side of that door were the two second-storey bedrooms, each with a balcony. A row of Izabela grapes supported by steel poles and wire stood to the right of the driveway when you drove up to the house. The front terrace,

the stairs on the left of the house that led past a row of lavender to the back terrace, and the entire façade, were all made
of cream-coloured granite. The roof was covered by brown
slate. On the back terrace was a free-standing stone barbecue and pizza oven, roof not finished yet, but a motor already
built in to turn a steel bar and roast a pig. On both front and
back terraces were massive round granite tables and benches.
At first, I thought they were ugly but then I recognized how
useful they were, how they didn't shift when you leaned on
them and how you could put a hot pot directly on them without a trivet. Other things around the house caught my eye, like
the brass faucet on the back terrace in the shape of a rooster.
Inside, in the wine cellar, were three steel barrels and a thick
wooden table hewn from a single massive teak tree and elk
antlers on the wall from a hunt in British Columbia and an
oak wine barrel that had once belonged to Marko's father on
which was inscribed, in Croatian, "If you drink you die, if you
don't drink you die, better drink then die."

For me, an important quality of the house wasn't what it
was made of or what it contained, but how its spaces were
connected to time, and how that determined how I spent my
time, how it channelled and shaped my experiences. Because
it faced the east, the front patio had the sun of the early morning and the back one had the shade. In the morning I sat in
the back taking in the first sounds of the day and breathing
in the still dewy smell of morning, the mixed together smell
of grass and flowers and herbs around the place, dandelions,
red clover, chamomile, yarrow, sage, wormwood. By lunch the
sun passed to the rear of the house, and the front terrace was
in the shade, so we occasionally ate our midday meal there
as the shadow cast by the house progressively descended the
sloping hill towards the road. By early evening, when the
sun still hung over the hill and the back terrace was still an
inferno, after I returned from a walk, I sat out front with a
beer, some bread and smoked špek and just enjoyed the warm

breezes, the view down the valley, the buzzing of the last bees in the lavender. By 7:30, the evening sun had slipped behind the hill so the back terrace was in the shade again and I would sit on one of the benches, the granite filled up with the day's hot sunshine even as the sun was beginning to set and the grass was growing moist from the dew, the night settling on the land; or I would water the vegetable garden with a hose from one of the big plastic canisters or watch the last swallows cutting up the back yard with their manoeuvres or wait for the bells from Marija Magdalena. And in the period between sunset and dark I read on the back terrace, a peaceful time for me when I didn't have to talk to anyone, and sometimes what I read seemed part of the moment in which I was living, and the place too, like Mink Snopes ploughing the land during the hot day and digging the fence posts for Jack Houston at night, walking beside woodlands of wild plum and beside planted fields standing strongly with corn, and dreaming for sure of an evening like this one, on his own land, his own place. When it got too dark to read, the bats appeared swooping floppily around the orchard. Then it was time to go in. Later, when everyone was asleep, I slipped outside again with a glass of šljivovica and stood there under the stars and the white moon, drinking in the sweet-smelling air and listening to the crickets, the hot summer earth boiling with life. . . .

I dreaded it but I knew I had to do it. So I had Joe strap me into the weed whacker and I headed up the hill. At first, I was all geared up with goggles and earmuffs but then ditched them both because of the heat and just went with the straw hat. I did poorly at first, kept knocking the head too hard on the ground and stretching out the wire. Joe yelled at me from below. But then I got into the rhythm. Long smooth arcs, the arcs of a peasant scything grass. My thoughts went back to Štefek cutting grass on this very hill and around his yard in the evenings with the wicker basket on his back, while I

kicked a soccer ball by myself. The smooth sound of the blade through the grass. The quiet of it. How unlike the loud revving of this machine that you could hear from half a kilometre away. That was a major difference in Srebrnjak these days: the snarl of a machine disturbing the quiet. I cut the grass in the orchard, then moved higher up. The land steepened viciously so that it was hard to keep my footing. My lower back started to ache from bending and swinging back and forth. My feet and ankles hurt from trying to keep my balance in my father's boots, which were some cheapos he'd bought in China, and had no ankle support. I was sweating and thirsty. My body wasn't what it was when I came to Srebrnjak, that much I recognized. I could see too how my father wasn't going to work on this hill much longer. How did men here keep doing it into their seventies? And by hand? I had personal experience scything and knew how hard it was. Finally the wire snagged on a branch and broke off completely and I was happy to use that as an excuse to go back down.

FIGURE 17. Tony Fabijančić scything grass in Srebrnjak, ca. 2013. Photograph by Denise Fabijančić.

"That's it?" Joe asked when he saw me. "You just started!"

"What do you mean just started?" I said. "I was up there a couple hours!"

"Fifteen minutes, tops," he said.

"You were on the couch watching TV; you lost track of time. Plus, the wire broke. Maybe if your gear was better, I'd still be up there."

"Oh sure."

I wrestled myself out of the harness, threw my wet shirt and socks into the sun, and asked, "What time is it?"

Joe looked at his watch. "Eleven."

"Shit. We're behind."

"That's riiiggghhht, you should have started earlier."

We had agreed to have a barbecue for our midday meal, which we ate at one as was the custom here. We got kindling together and started a fire in the outdoor oven and I drove to Samobor for the meat. The single-lane highway between Sveta Nedelja and Samobor, which had until now been made of concretes slabs built by the Germans, the area where Slavko had told me the Partisans had hanged men after the war, was covered by new blacktop. But the big change was the new enterprise. On the Sveta Nedelja end was Croatian car manufacturer Rimac Automobil, founded in 2009 by then twenty-one-year-old Mate Rimac, a precocious car genius who produced one of the world's fastest production electrical vehicles, the Concept One. On the Samobor end of the highway were all the new grocery stores. Kaufland, Lidl, Plodine and Croatia's own Konzum. What a difference from the early post-Yugoslavia days when a country corner store or two seemed like a profusion of capitalist enterprise. For me, the choices of my favourites were astonishing: hundreds of double-smoked bacons, hams, dried smoked sausages, cheeses from Croatia, Germany and Austria, walls stacked with different beers from Croatia and Europe (all the labels, all the beautiful coloured glass!), Ožujsko, Karlovačko, Osječko,

Tomislav, Zmajska pivovara, Pan, Laško, and the usual big names like Heineken, Beck's, Warsteiner, Erdinger, Paulaner, Holsten, Kaltenberg, Budweiser Budvar, Staropramen, you name it, some now in two-litre pop bottles (but not a single brand from North America), and not to mention inexpensive white *graševina* from Slavonia, four bucks a bottle, and red Plavac Mali from the coast, and the Williams pear, plum, and herb brandies. But I had no time to hang around, so I got the chicken legs and *čevapi* sausages and went back to Srebrnjak.

Joe had been tending the fire in my absence and the embers were about right when I returned, so we put the meat on the grill. The sun was beating hard on our heads (this was before he had finished the roof of the pizza oven). I had to make some trips downstairs for a longer fork and a bowl of olive oil and a brush to baste the chicken, going up and down the stairs beside the row of swaying lavender, the bees droning, and small white butterflies dancing around the purple tops. I watched Joe turn the meat. I remembered him barbecuing on our backyard patio in Edmonton, barbecuing that Alberta steak.

"In Alberta steak is two inches thick," I said out loud.

"That's right," Joe answered, "they know what they're doing over there."

He wasn't following my thoughts. I said, "Steak two inches thick and jobs five bucks an hour, hey Tonček, you gotta come!"

Joe laughed. "Well, he listened, didn't he?"

"I bet he was happy with you!"

"He made the right decision in the end."

I wasn't so sure. "He left France and came to Edmonton, so what do you think is better?"

"He's a millionaire now."

"Yes, but he woulda worked there too. Plus, there he could wear a suit jacket and leather shoes in the winter. You're the first person to understand that. And there were other reasons to stick around. Young stud in his prime, you know. . . ."

"Maybe."

"He followed you all the way from Srebrnjak to Edmonton, Alberta. Escaped Yugoslavia as well. Just eighteen years old. He told me about that once. Walking in the night on a deer trail through the mountains. Quite a story."

We went on for a while discussing Tonček's decision. Then the meat was ready, and we went down to the table on the front terrace. The shade from the house and a light easterly wind made it cool compared to the back. Joe brought his wine from the *podrom,* and Denise the potatoes and salad, and we ate. A few wasps showed up and we shooed them away. Three grey cats that lived at Mila's appeared, waiting expectantly in the bushes. It was 1:30. With my back to the house I had a view of the big hill across the street, the Izabela grapes and drive-way on the left, Štefek's barn below and, farther to the right, the well under the walnut tree. If I walked down the slop-ing hill to the well and then under the tree, I would end up in Mila's yard. If I turned around there and faced my father's house and looked up to where I was eating now, I would see the vineyard on the hill high on the left, the one my grandfather and his brothers planted in the early twentieth century, now Miško's, and to the right, even higher, the vineyard Štefek had planted, which belonged now to the loudmouth son-in-law who had taken the apple meant for my grandmother in 1977. All this was part of my positional awareness as we ate.

When we were done, we sat there longer, Joe and I. It was a hot, bright afternoon. Above, a hawk hung slow turns onto the cloudless blue sky. Doves cooed sleepily. No other sound. No weed whacker to ruin the silence. People were waiting for it to cool off. I looked down at Mila's barn and pictures sud-denly ghosted through my mind, one layered on the other like double exposures—of the family moving through the yard working; of Mila walking to the barn to milk the cows; of Strina Slava picking nettles; and of the pig roasts under the plum trees, people gathered, their shapes flitting here and there, gathered together for a photo. I saw myself running from the hill for a drink of water from the pail and then going into the barn and coming out grown up and heading off down the road on the black bike to the sound of Mila's, "Kuda, Tony?" And then a change of light and returning in the dark searching for the key on the windowsill, heart beating hard, those dogs. . . .

"Štefek would be out there hoeing corn now, wouldn't he?" I asked Joe. Five years had passed since Štefek had died, but we hadn't spoken much about him.

"Maybe he would be hoeing, but even he knew when to cool it. He got smarter when he got older."

"I saw him going up the hill right over there, him and that hoe. More than once. Hot like this. A whole field of it waiting for him."

"That's riiigggghhht! And you complain about weeding a little garden, sonny boy."

"And always ahead of Mila."

"To make it easier for her, probably."

"Just imagine the boredom of it," I said, "hour after hour."

"Maybe he didn't find it boring. Not everyone finds work boring, you know. Not everyone is like you. But that's what he did, he worked. There was always something. Even here there is no end to it. He had to work or he would go hungry. Simple. And you know he had other options. After the war he could have had a career in the military. The communists wanted him. They kept writing him with offers. The police wanted him. He could have been chief of police in Sveta Nedelja. He would have had benefits."

"Earned more money."

"Maybe more money, but for sure an easier life. But he refused."

"Why did he do that?"

"There were all these promises. The communists made all these promises after the war.

We will have freedom. Everyone will be free. Brotherhood and Unity. All this crapperoo.

He was a Partisan in the war, and maybe he believed it all. For a while he believed it all. Then his brother was arrested and nearly hanged. For nothing. My mother helped save his life. He would have been hanged otherwise."

"So you're saying he started to have doubts."

"He just gave up on all that. He had principles."

"I remember there was never a picture of Tito in the house, not that I ever saw."

"None of that, no Jesus either. And there is something else. When I was small, I saw this. It was in the bedroom; I was young, maybe five years old. It was coming to the morning, and he had a dream. It woke me up. He started to scream. He was screaming about being bombarded. We all had to run because we were being bombarded. He jumped up and jumped out of the window. It was summer, I think. Then he woke up and he was back to normal. He didn't have another of those episodes, not that I saw."

"You didn't see everything," I said. "For sure he was going through this shit all the time, and who knows how long it lasted."

"Maybe forever."

"Maybe forever."

"You can talk about what he gave up when you start to write," my father said. "I remember this too. After the war, he worked at *Top*, the aluminum factory in Kerestinec. He walked there and he walked back. He was too poor for a bicycle yet. The bike was later. But at that time he had to walk. After work he went to buy a loaf of bread at the bakery by the factory. In those days we couldn't use up our corn for bread. There was always a lineup by the time he showed up. Sometimes he waited an hour for a loaf of bread before coming back home. He could have had one waiting for him with the right connections. If he had joined the communists, you better believe someone

— 119 —

would have been there with a loaf for him. He would have had connections. He *chose* to wait instead."

"Made a decision that he was going to wait and then stuck with it."

"That's right. And he never got a military pension either."

"Maybe he regretted that."

"Maybe. You make decisions and stick with them. He knew how to work, that's for sure. He was up every morning at four to feed the animals and then to walk to work. Then when he came home, he ate and then continued to work on the land. That vineyard up there. Not my father's, the other one. He dug it by himself, dug the trenches for the vines by himself."

"Imagine the sheer physical hardness of that. Holy shit," I said.

"There's something else too," my father added. "He used to beat me. For this and that. I can't say I was perfect, I know that. But he hit me. Even across the head. I was just a kid. My brother Dragec told him if he did again, he was going to kill him. Dragec was maybe thirteen or fourteen. Said he would kill him if he did it again. And you know what? He never did."

"So maybe that is why Štefek didn't like handouts from you, like when you gave him money to put in the washroom upstairs."

"Could be. He was ashamed possibly."

A whole other side of Štefek had suddenly appeared to me. The person I'd known had turned out to be just the front part of the man, in back of which were the hidden things. His relentless work now took on a different meaning. The anger in the barn with the cows. The separation from others. How much else was there? How long did the war last in his thoughts? Even Mila might not have known all of it.

Joe had never told me the story of his brother Dragec warning Štefek. Joe's full brother, "Charlie" as he became known in North America, had left Srebrnjak in the 1960s and had never returned. Not coming back was an indictment of a place and people that had always seemed peaceful and decent to me. Charlie, more than his two brothers, seemed to bear the consequences of his mother's abandonment the most, caving in to all the addictions over the years except drugs, and never returning to his home until his ashes were buried in the grave under the black granite headstone Joe had put in the cemetery in Sveta Nedelja. No one in Srebrnjak ever brought up Charlie's name. In one of my conversations with him over the phone (he called every two years or so from some city in America—at first San Diego, then San Francisco, then Chicago, then Reno at the end)—his rough American voice told me about the whippings he and Joe had gotten. He said, "Mila was a bad person." He didn't go into more detail. But there was a bitterness and hatred there. He spared both Jana and Strina Slava, whom he called a "great woman." However, with the others there was no burying the hatchet. He'd never felt at home with them in Srebrnjak. He had other reasons for not going back too. He rarely had enough ready cash to buy a ticket after the casino and the booze. Plus, he hated the communists who still ran the country. In another conversation, Charlie shared his views of the world with me. "They think they're educated; they think they know something," he said once, "those people with their university degrees, but you know fuck all. Being a machinist like me takes just as much intelligence. Don't think it doesn't. I always think, calculate, when I work." I thought his remarks were partly directed at me. "Whatever you say, buddy," I answered testily. I always felt bad about that. He was for sure a proud person. And forceful too. That was obvious even when he was a kid. The man who had lost two fingers to the axe in Srebrnjak, Tonček Juranko, told me how Charlie had taught him chess. "We used to play in the barn loft. If I made a mistake, he got up and leaned over and slapped me across the face. Wham! Then later, if I made another mistake, he got up and slapped me again! Holy shit! Did I ever learn fast!"

Joe and I sat there for a while longer, then I went to my room for a rest. I lowered the shutters, took off my shirt and tried to nap. It was hot, 39 degrees outside, that's what the thermometer read by the pizza oven, so that even on this level of the house, with another storey above, I was sweating. Now and again I heard Marica's rooster crowing lazily down at Mila's place. A car down on the road. I was thinking about what we'd been talking about and then I must have slept because an hour had gone by when I woke up.

Downstairs, Joe, who had napped on the couch, the TV still blaring, had just gotten up and was in the garage with a spade in his hand.

"You came just in time," he laughed.

"What do you mean?"

"Here let me show you." He went over to the grapes. "See here." He began to dig at the earth between the vines. "This has to be done."

"What do you mean? It's a hundred degrees outside and you want to *kopati*."

"It's shady now. This digging has to be done. Look at the weeds."

He was right about the shade. Some of the grapes were in the shadow of the house at this time of the day. I took the spade and dug half-heartedly. He kept his eyes on me.

"Turn the soil over, there's no point if the weeds stay inside. You're not doing anything. Here, give me that, watch now. See how I'm doing it." He took the spade and began to dig, stepping under the grapes to get at the earth on the other side. He made sure not to spill soil onto the driveway.

"I do see," I said. "You're doing great! You're good at it. Keep going, keep showing me how to do it properly."

He gave me a wicked smile. Then he kept going. "Like this," he said. He had got to the point where he was in the sun and as he kept turning over the soil he started to sweat. He stopped and looked at me and laughed. "Pheww, it's hot."

"Obviously it's hot. Give it up for today. *Mañana*, man. You're not wearing a hat either. One of these days you're going to have a problem. Do you want to have a beer? Come and have a beer."

We sat out front with our beers. It was cooling down a little, and the shadow from the house was halfway to the barn. The sky was a darker blue, the hawk now gone. No sound broke the thick stillness of the early evening. A man was coming up the hill on the land beside the house. We saw it was the son-in-law pushing a wheelbarrow to his garden. I said hello and he waved back with a nod and said hello but kept going.

"There he goes," I said.

"Oh shit," Joe said, laughing, "Just the other day he came over here," he pointed to the land on the other side of his house, just beyond his grapes. "His apricot tree is close to the property line and the branches hang over onto this side. The apricots fall onto this side. So he came over and cut the branches down. He left the apricots on the ground because he knew he couldn't touch them now, but he decided no more were going to fall on our land. That tells you all you need to know."

"He and his wife are here every day now," he went on. "Working harder now than they ever did."

"They used to pick up supplies at Mila's groceteria, and now they're working for it."

"That's right."

"Why do you think?"

"No idea, maybe they need to."

"Pretty much the only people working on the land in Srebrnjak. Other than Marica and Miško, plus there's Tomo and his wife. That's about it."

Srebrnjak had for sure changed, Joe said. "It's going back to what it used to be. There weren't many peasants then. Rich people from Samobor and Zagreb owned much of the land before the wars, even after. They had vineyards. They would come for the weekends. They hired peasants to do the work.

The Špišička family from Samobor. Their house is still here, just up the road in the trees."

I think I knew what he was talking about. I remembered the winter of 1992 and the old house that had become visible from the road because the trees had lost their leaves. Joe went on to tell me that the daughter of the family who had inherited all the land, had fallen on hard times and had sold the land piece by piece until there was nothing left. A once wealthy family reduced to nothing. "She drove a taxi for a while. A big Mercedes. The colour of champagne. There wasn't much money in it. No one could afford a bike let alone a taxi ride."

"What happened to her?"

"No idea."

"She might have gone into another line of work."

"Maybe."

He told me the story of rich people coming into the valley during the winter. They drove horse-drawn sleighs on the winter-solid roads and spent time in their cottages. Once, when he was walking to school with his brother, Charlie, or possibly his cousin in Dol, the other Štefek Juranko, he wasn't sure any longer, a rich man drove past on his sleigh. "We were going to school in Sveta Nedelja and we had two more kilometres to walk. We asked him for a ride. You know, to sit on the back of the sleigh. He wouldn't let us. He said the extra weight would be a burden to the horse!"

"A total asshole!" I said.

"Complete."

"Bet he forgot about you. But you remember him!"

"That's right. We were just some poor nobodies."

"And you were kids. But you still understood how he looked at you. That's why you remember."

"That's right."

"Buddy never would have imagined his decision on that road would end up being talked about seventy years later! Serves him right."

"Yes."

He told me that during this postwar period, he and his brother had only one pair of boots. Going to school in the spring and fall, he would wear one boot, Charlie the other, then they would switch halfway.

We talked for a while longer. Later, I fetched my book and read on the back terrace. Joe went around with the hose watering the plants. It was cooling off finally, the sun having dipped beneath the hill. One of the cats was on the hill hunting for mice and a few last birds were flying about and twittering in the trees. Crickets chirping in the orchard. It was a beautiful sound, especially just after I'd arrived and not having heard it for so long.

After the bells from Marija Magdalena tolled, when the light started to go out of the day, I went down to Mila's. She liked it when someone came to visit her at night before bed. By now she was expecting a nightly visit from Joe or Denise. Left the door unlocked and waited in the kitchen. She felt less alone in the empty house. Seven years had gone by since I'd last been here, saying goodbye outside the front door after Štefek had shown me the footings of Joe's house, and when I went into Mila's house I smelled the dank concrete again and wine from the cellar. The house no longer smelled of milk and cheese as it did in 1969.

She was sitting at the kitchen table watching TV. At first, I wasn't sure it was her. She had lost weight, her face was gaunt, and the lenses of her glasses were dark, giving her the appearance of a blind woman. She didn't recognize me at first either.

"Tony!" she finally said.

"Mila!" I answered.

"Tony!"

"Milaaaaa!"

She laughed. "What is it?"

"Nothing. I've come."

"I know that."

"Didn't you recognize me?"

"Tony, listen, I can't see out of this eye, it's like a fog, and the other one isn't much better. I know it's you, I can see it's you, but you're not very clear."

"That's not good."

"It's not good, but what can you do? What can a person do? There's nothing to do."

"Yes," I said, "But you can't look at it that way. I told Oma all the time, I told her at least she had her eyesight when she had lost her sense of smell and taste. At least she had that. She could watch TV or talk with people or whatever. You have to look at the bright side."

"There is no bright side."

There was no reasoning with her. I thought of the story Joe had told me about her and her eyesight. "Joža said you asked him the other day where he was going in the car. And he said to you, 'Hey Mila, how could you tell it was me if you're blind like you say you are?'"

"I knew it was his car by the colour. He drives a white car."

"You're right, he does drive a white car."

"I could see the colour and I knew it was him."

I turned the subject to Joe, something other than herself, and her mood improved. The old sarcastic Mila reappeared.

"Hey Mila," I said, "I came yesterday and saw the house, and let me tell you it is one big place."

"Too big," she said, "you could put an army in that house!"

"But he wouldn't listen. I told him, but he never listened."

"Why would he listen," she said, "when he knows everything himself. Even when he was a boy, he knew everything better. He was always smarter. Oh yes, so smart!"

We had a laugh at that.

"Mila, listen, I came here and almost first thing he has me working on the hill. Can you believe it? Up on the hill cutting grass. It was hot."

"Tony, listen, you didn't come here for that. You are a professor, not a peasant. What are you doing that for? If he wants the work done, let him do it himself."

"That's right, let him do it himself."

We went on to talk of various things, going back in time as we often did. She told me that the woman who had called me crazy for running in the hills back in 1987 was none other than Kata Deak, the youngest sister of Draga Husta, who still lived in Mala Gorica. Mila described how Marko had come in the night and knocked on her door, having escaped his house through a window; this was after Štefek had died and she was alone. She said that whatever had happened to Marko was karma for what he had done to his own father, how he had maltreated him. She didn't go into details, and she didn't use the word "karma." What you sow is what you reap. Then she turned her lens onto herself again, said with sudden bitterness, her face looking away from me for the first time, her voice low, self-pitying, "What a waste all this was, this life here. I could have done more, learned something. Instead I ended up here. With a man like him." She was rubbing her fingers together anxiously. Looking into space as though she were alone. The TV was on, some variety show with people singing and dancing, which we weren't paying attention to. She had never talked to me like this before. A window had suddenly opened into her mind and what I saw was dark. She couldn't see much anymore with her eyes, but she was looking all the way into herself. Even now as I write I think of her as the tough, practical Mila whose view of life was unemotional, clear and unambiguous, without doubt, the one who told me straight and without hesitation, when I said once that I was contemplating sleeping on a bench in the airport to save money on a hotel, "You're not an animal, sleep like a human." For years I had an idea of who Mila was—the woman who had fed me and had long talks with me and gossiped with me, laughed with me, who had helped raise my father, who worked hard every day but never liked it (now I had a better idea why). For years this was the woman to whom I remained loyal even as others slandered her by saying she was bad or crazy. Even as she became the gossip of others, the tables having turned, when she went into the podrom and pulled on the son-in-law's wine barrel after he'd refused to drive her up Joe's driveway to his house, a difficult walk for her in the heat but also an odd request, he saying he was too busy, though no one knows for certain that is why she did it, why she pulled over his wine barrel and lay on the concrete floor in the wine, lying there on the cold wine-covered floor until she was found the next morning incoherent, then mute about it all, so that even as she became the gossip of others, I remained loyal to the Mila of my choice.

Now this veiled comment of hers about Štefek set me back on my heels, especially after my conversation that afternoon with Joe. I had reassessed Štefek once, and now I was having to do it again. My eyes went to the floor by the wood box where he had fallen dead that morning in 2008, when she'd come downstairs and saw him and went blind in one eye. I thought of the relentless, distant, sometimes angry man. Later Joe told me that Mila had asked him to be buried in his grave rather than her husband's. And then I learned that Mila had told Denise a terrible secret about her life, swore her to secrecy, told her that Štefek had done something terrible to her, that it involved her own mother, but swore her to secrecy. . . .

A few weeks went by. Near the end of my stay, for the first time in many years, I travelled to the coast again. I was glad to leave the north behind, the heavy human drama, all the history. None of that would exist for me on the islands I was going to.

And yet I couldn't go completely in peace. My wife had given me a hard look when I told her I was planning another travel writing excursion for my third such book. It was a look of disdain like the one she had given me when we first met on the road in Brezje as she was roller-skating and I was driving my "Mercedes."

"More of your piddly scribbling?" she asked. "Bothering people you don't even know. Why don't you write a novel instead? Why don't you write a bestseller that will help your family? Why don't you think of your family like a real husband?" I answered that Joe was going to come with me on the trip, knowing that his presence would soften my wife's bitterness because she knew all too well that I had only so much time remaining with my not so young father, and that every opportunity missed might be a source of remorse later.

I admit I didn't have her words in mind when I approached Cres by ferry as the sun went down and the old familiar thrill went through me when I saw the sea and the islands again.

As our boat approached, Cres rose high and dark, covered by oak woods. We climbed a twisting road from the terminal and drove to the town of Cres at dusk, past a thousand blue olive groves, grey ribbons of rock walls hundreds of metres long, stone sheds, and wooden fences to keep in sheep, so that the island in these parts, open to the darkening sky, wildly ominous and empty, reminded me of Pag in spots.

We found a place to stay in the town of Cres. Then we made for a restaurant down the street, close enough for Joe, a lazy walker, and settled down for a meal on a terrace open to the night sky. The clacking of cicadas surrounded us. Gone were the crickets of the north. The evening air was dryer and warmer than in Srebrnjak and smelled of the sea, flowers, and garlic.

An Italian family was sitting at a long table when we arrived. They were among the Italian crowds who came to Cres on the weekends early in the season, then flooded the island for longer stretches during high summer. An elderly German couple, long-time visitors judging by their meeting with the owner, arrived. The owner seemed enthused about their return, kissing them on the cheeks, tapping the old man's arm, but his superficial verbal exchange and reticence about himself made him seem in fact distant and uninterested. He went to bring them wine and they began to smoke. Smoking had been prohibited at restaurants, but here, at a place where they had evidently spent a lot of money over the years, there was no stopping the old habits.

When the owner came to our table, he ditched some of the formality with which he'd greeted the others, maybe because he considered us Croats like him and could speak to us in his first language, though he did say he had learned Italian as a boy. He told us about the island, lowering his voice discreetly when he mentioned the Italian fascists who had settled in Valun during the Second World War. He gave us advice about what to see on Cres. "You must go to Beli, yes, and Lubenice, but Beli is a must."

The menu was in four languages, Croatian, Italian, German and English. We ordered a mixed dish of squid, *škampi* and mussels, which was served generously on a large platter, and washed it down with Ožujsko beer, followed at the end with two jiggers of šljivovica, on the house. The boss knew what to do to bring us back! The Italians continued to talk, the Germans to smoke, and we sat there for a while longer as music played and a half moon moved through the black branches. Then we got up and went back to our apartment.

The town of Cres is an attractive pastel-façaded bit of Italy that reminded me of Rovinj and Pag combined, but after exploring it briefly, we took the waiter's advice and drove the twenty-three kilometres north to the mountaintop village of Beli. The narrow, rough road gave us views on the right of the glittering surface of the Adriatic, cross-hatched as it is when you look at roughened seawater from a plane. Beyond that we saw the island of Krk and the blue-green mainland behind. The one-lane road wound on through deep woods of oak, chestnut, hornbeam and elm, shaded and peaceful, with spots of light dancing through the thick cover. We passed rock walls so close to the road that we had to come to a standstill when other cars approached. Finally, after an hour or so, we arrived in Beli.

A raucous thrumming of cicadas in the trees around the village met us when we got out. The street that led up into the village was like a hilly path made of round mortared stones, slick, shiny and uneven. The village was built high on the northern side of the island, so that

FIGURE 18. Street in Beli, island of Cres, 2013

every contour of the land dictated the cant of the streets and position of houses. The farther in I walked the more I felt enclosed by the gloom of time having passed the village by. There were abandoned houses peeling blue and pink paint, with closed shutters and decrepit iron balconies that now seemed sad and pathetically ornate. But there was life too; I heard voices through open windows, smelled fish frying in a kitchen. Grapes and wisteria hung on trellises throughout the village, flowers stood in rows outside doors, oleanders, begonias and others not native to the coast, rosemary and bay leaf in small pots. One alley led through a wooden gate down a steep trail to a beach at the base of the mountain. Almost invisible, tacked high onto the blue sky, was a bird, possibly a rare griffon vulture, but too far away for me to be sure.

In the centre of Beli was a church, a tall tree casting quiet shade, a well, and a stone trough. The well was no longer used, and the square was empty. We were about to move on when an elderly man showed up, seeming to have arrived for no particular reason, and pretending not to look at us, yet somehow watching us with interest. He wore a white т-shirt, shorts, and rubber beach shoes. My father thought it would be a good idea to talk to him, a local who would tell us about his village. When I addressed him in Croatian, to our surprise, he answered in English. English with a Croatian and American accent. "I'm from Croatia, but I been in States last fifty years. Chicago and Boca Raton. This was my wife's house, my wife's parent's house, but now they're gone. My wife she died three years ago, so there's only me. I come to Beli every summer. Then I go back. I used to go back to Florida, but I'm comin' over here for good. I gotta apartment in Rijeka. Tomorrow gotta go back to Rijeka for business ('beesness,' he pronounced it). My accountant he's sendin' me a fax about how my stocks are doin'."

His name was Vladimir Ingrec and he was eighty-five years old. He was a big man with still lively eyes and thick legs that had long scars along the side of the knees. "Wanna see my place?" He pulled out a key, unlocked the front door of the house, or apartment, and showed us inside. There was a new kitchen, a washer/dryer, and stairs leading to bedrooms upstairs, which he didn't invite us to see. Across the square was another place that had belonged to his mother-in-law's side of the family. It was danker and more run-down than his own, had eerie black-and-whites of long dead family members, a row of silver Turkish coffee cups on top of a cupboard, and cramped low-ceilinged bedrooms on the second floor above creaky stairs.

Outside in daylight again Vladimir invited us for a beer at the beach. We walked down the bumpy street to the car, and I marvelled at his confidence on the stones, even though he teetered at times. We drove down the steep road to the beach and sat at a picnic table on the terrace with a crowd of young beachgoers. Most of them were here for a few days or weeks, just passing through. Some young guys said hello to him, the waitress was on familiar terms with him, and he ordered the latest citron-flavoured Ožujsko.

"I swim here every day," Vladimir said, pointing to the white line of buoys across the cove. "There and back, that's enough for someone like me. I was good athlete. I played tennis back in U.S. They called me 'Destroyer' 'cause I was big force on tennis court. Nothing could stop me. The only thing could stop me was my knees. I had surgery on both, look at this." He showed us his scars. "That slowed me up, but I kept on playing, up to I was seventy-seven."

He started to talk about his wife. "My wife she was great woman, beautiful person. What a lady! We got married fifty years ago, same summer we went to States. We married in church here in Beli. The priest who did the ceremony he was still alive last summer, ninety-six years old. He remembered me. He died this summer, and I went to his funeral. But as I was saying, my wife and me, we went to America. First, we took boat to Halifax, and then train to Montréal. It was something, it was beautiful, we made love, my wife and me, in the cabin of the train in the night." He laughed at the memory, and we laughed too. "I still have her wedding dress. I brought it back from the States. It's in my apartment in Rijeka. Something to remember. I don't really look at it." He went on for a while recalling the past as the beach crowd came and went at the bar, and the light began to change. I felt sorry about it, but we had to go.

"I gotta go too. I'm leavin' for Rijeka tomorrow. My accountant he's sendin' me a fax about my stocks, so I gotta tell him what I want him to do. I'm gonna swim and then go back. The taxi comes at five tomorrow." I asked if he wanted a ride back up, but he said he would find someone here, there was always someone, and then we waved goodbye and left him.

We went to the mountaintop village of Lubenice on the western side of Cres as the daylight started to fade, the sun sending its last warm light over the western ridge of the island, on rock walls, sheep huts, copses of low evergreens and other trees that dotted the stony fields. There were a few oak tree sections, but the landscape looked aridly Mediterranean. We'd thought the road to Beli was tricky, but the one to Lubenice was worse. More of a paved bike path than a road, it snuck slyly through forests and dry grass meadows, insidiously throwing out blind curves as though it were trying to delay us. Walls crowded the road, the pavement was very narrow, so when cars approached we had to pull in both mirrors.

"Slow, here, sonny boy" Joe warned. "SLOOWWWW down!"

"I AM slowing down! What does it look like I'm doing?" I shouted back. "If you were driving you would have scraped the hell out of the sides by now!"

"Sure, sure," he answered. Luckily, makeshift patches of concrete had been laid down at various places to create more room. Even so, what should have been a ten-minute drive from the "main" road, five kilometres distant, took us much longer.

We arrived as the sun was setting. An agglomeration of stone buildings on cliffs high above the sea, Lubenice was founded some 4,000 years ago. More hamlet than village, its streets were bumpy rock and grass paths with no names. In contrast, Beli seemed like a city.

I got out of the car and walked into the village, past the big parish church and other chapels. There seemed to be more churches than people. Sitting on a concrete bench, leaning on her cane, was an old woman wearing black, the sort I had seen in Pag years back. Through an archway I passed into the northern part of the village where there were little vegetable gardens, some right on the cliff edge, chicken coops, patches of marigolds and foundations of long-gone houses. I peered down and saw a crescent-shaped beach far below. The few tourists who had wandered around Lubenice had left and

I was alone now. The wind rose from the sea, bending the golden grass and driving the last clouds to the darkening east. I imagined the same wind in wintertime, howling through chinks in the stone houses, but now there was heat still in the sun and the light tinged the buildings and the grass with gold.

On the way back to the car I stopped at a former school and library that had been turned into a gallery. The young caretaker of the gallery, twenty-five-year-old Romano Faganel, spent most

FIGURE 19. Home in Lubenice, island of Cres, 2013

of the summer here, sleeping in the loft. He had no running water or electricity and ate with a family in the village. His wages were paid by the Cres tourist board, but they were probably a pittance. "I don't mind. I didn't come here for the money. I wanted to experience Lubenice like this, like it must have been."

The shelves had books in Croatian and some in English, like Alistair MacLean's *South by Java Head,* a book I owned and read as a boy. On the walls were photographs of the village and its remaining aged residents, who numbered five or six. The pictures from the previous winter were taken after a snowstorm, and where today there was tall grass, gardens, and marigolds, in the winter there was snow ten centimetres deep. The transformation of Lubenice from an Adriatic seaside village to a wintry alpine one was incredible. "You see, Cres is farther north than other Croatian islands. If you go just a few kilometres south, to Lošinj, you have a sub-tropical climate. There the temperature is two or three degrees warmer. There is always difference in sea temperature." I looked at the rest of the photos, the snow-covered Mediterranean evergreen maquis, a covered chapel roof, an old man gathering winter fuel.

Before leaving I donated twenty kuna to a Cres eco-tourism association and got a wooden pin. We stepped outside into the last sun and the warm blustery wind. I shook hands with Romano and returned to Joe. He had walked around a bit, which told me he had found something in Lubenice worth seeing.

"Quite a place, isn't it?" I said.

"Quite a place."

Next day we arrived at the southern tip of Cres, which used to be joined with the island of Lošinj until the Romans dug a channel at the end of the third century BCE. We came to the small town of Osor, where there was a rotating bridge to let water traffic through. During the Roman period, 15,000 people lived here; now there were sixty. Still, with its straight cobbled streets, its finial architectural touches and its garden delights, like a tall red blooming oleander tree growing out of the cobbles near the main square, and flowers in ceramic pots on sills outside windows whose trims were painted bright blue, Osor projected the feeling of a town, not a village.

We sat at a café in the middle of Osor. A truck had backed up to the terrace and delivery men were dropping off containers of beer. Some June bugs were flying around clumsily. Other than that, not much was happening. We were tired still from the long day before, and I sat there absently while Joe drank his usual morning coffee. He picked up a newspaper, then put it down and said, "This government has to go." I thought he knew something about Osor I didn't, its municipal politics or something along those line, but he was referring to the national government led by then Prime Minister Zoran Milanović. A favourite topic of his.

"How did you get onto that track?"

"I'm reading about more stupidity. It reminded me of something the prime minister said a year ago."

"What was that?"

"He called Croatia an "accidental country!"

"Accidental country?"

"That's riiiigghhht." He gave me a wicked smile. "It happened by accident. Just happened, no one did anything."

"Out of the blue," I said.

"Out of the blue, that's right. No one fought, no one died. This tells you where his mentality is about Croatia, it tells you a lot. For a prime minister to say this about his own country, this is serious business. Seerrriooousss."

There were several layers to what Joe was saying, but it boiled down to the idea that the prime minister didn't appear to agree with the story told by Croats about the birth of their nation in the '90s, its defeat of Yugo army-led Serbian insurgents in eastern Slavonia and the Krajina, and so on.

"The prime minister is not a nationalist," I said.

"Not a nationalist. He's a communist, the old communist party. They just changed the name."

"So why did Croatians vote for him?"

"Who knows? The other party was corrupt. He dressed himself up, talked about joining the European Union."

"So, you can vote him out. His government will be finished. Power always comes to an end. In democracies or otherwise. Look at Osor," I said. "This town was big once, important. There were thousands living here."

"And some of them had power, you better believe it," Joe said.

"Not anymore!"

"Ha, not anymore."

So, after a brief stay on a beach in Veli Lošinj, we ended our trip to the northern Adriatic. However, that summer Joe and I also travelled to the far south and the island of Vis. For the first time ever, we drove down the new "superhighway" that allowed us to bypass the narrow Magistrala. This meant no more slow winding roads through Kordun and Lika, but also no more sights of small villages and women by the roadside selling their honey and cheese, no more views of the sea and the islands off dangerous cliffs. Of course, there wouldn't have been Roma with dancing bears any longer, either. The highway swept through the continental north then bore through the Velebit Mountains via the Mala Kapela and Sveti Rok tunnels and brought us out to the other side, where we saw the Adriatic far below. The rest of the route was through arid hinterland, Bosnia-Herzegovina to our left and the Velebit on our right.

The ferry from Split to Vis covered thirty nautical miles in two and a half hours, slipping through a narrow channel between Šolta and Brač called Splitska vrata ("Split doors") and then heading out to open sea where Hvar and Korčula floated in the distant mist. Thunderheads hung low over the Mosor mountains on the mainland, but at sea it was sunny, warm, and windy. Over the intercom a cheerful voice greeted us: "Welcome, visitors, to the Petar Hektorović. Welcome to the new Croatia! Yes, the new Croatia! We have finally entered Europe. However, the question is, when will we get out!?"

This comment produced that cynical cackle from Joe. The guy on the intercom was referring to Croatia's entry into the E.U., which not everyone in the country supported. The voice went on, quoting at length from the long poem by Petar Hektorović, *Ribanje I ribarsko prigovaranje* (*Fishing and Fishermen's Conversation*), and then signing off by saying, "This little message was brought to you by Pepe, Pepe from Komiža. *Do viđenja!*—Goodbye."

We stood on the upper deck as the ferry entered a very long narrow bay and approached the town of Vis. A warm wind buffeted us as the houses around the harbour slid past. A large, abandoned stone house was on the southern side. Joe remarked, "They left a long time ago, and not because of the last war." He meant that under the Yugoslav regime Vis was a military island closed to all foreigners until 1989. Locals couldn't profit from tourism as islanders could elsewhere, and many were motivated to leave for good.

Vis had the look of an old place, even more so than other Dalmatian towns. On the steep hills, former garden terraces and spaces where vineyards used to grow were visible. Clutches of cypresses, taller than the scruffy garrigue shrubbery, added to the impression of the classical antiquity of Vis.

As we waited in the lineup to get off the ferry, an elderly man with wine red cheeks and wild pitch-black hair that looked dyed approached our car and asked in English, "Did you enjoy your voyage? Did you enjoy the commentary? That was me, Pepe. I'm Pepe. Pepe from Komiža. If you need a place to stay, come to Pepe's apartments in Komiža." With that he whirled off into the crowd, yelling greetings to people he knew.

The road from Vis to Komiža was a new blacktop twisting across the mountainous spine of the island. The setting sun was in our eyes and lit the steep faces of the mountain, the stone piles and longish wall-like mounds that had been built up to clear the ground. There were no more vineyards, however, just the island's natural vegetation. After a while, though, Joe pointed to a tended vineyard, light green against the surrounding darker green, and said, "There, that gives you an idea of what it used to be like here." I could picture the face of the mountain covered by gardens and vineyards; I imagined the early settlers, the Greeks, then the Romans, in their distant age, wending up the path and clearing the rocks for hours in the catatonic afternoon sun, then trudging back down to the settlements and repeating it all the next day, and then those who carried on in the years afterwards working among the rows of vines, and then in late summer harvesting the grapes in baskets which they slung on either side of donkeys and transported down the winding paths. . . .

We arrived on the other side of the island. Komiža spills out below to the edges of a round bay of the same name. Signs for *sobe* and *camere* were everywhere, but nothing suited Joe (he thought Pepe's apartments would be too pricey). Then he noticed a cardboard sign on a wooden wine barrel that was printed in a rough hand advertising the prices for *vino, likeri*. The owner of the house was sitting in his small courtyard; he came to the gate when we stepped out of the car. His name was Srećko Božanić, a stocky seventy-three-year-old in a pressed white short-sleeved shirt, suspenders and khaki pants who walked with a cane. He led us to the cottage at the end of the courtyard. It had only one bed, and at first the memory of that freezing Christmas in Srebrnjak, when Joe and I had huddled under blankets together, put me off at first, but with no better options, I caved in.

Our host surprised us by bringing two shot glasses filled with a copper, slightly transparent liquid to our outdoor table. The liquor, *smokvica*, was sweet and tasted slightly like the figs from which it was made. We sat and talked to Srećko, who remained standing, one arm holding a tree branch, the other his cane. When we had finished our drinks, he brought us a tart lemon liquor, limoncello. The limoncello tasted light, fruity, and seemed to fit the season.

The drinks set us a good mood, so we decided to walk to the harbour. The street descended for two hundred metres and was made of knobbly stones mortared together with long slabs that sagged from years of walkers' steps. Komiža's crooked meandering streets, unlike Pag's, hadn't been repaved for many years. Most of the buildings in this old quarter were constructed out of beige, unfaçaded blocks, which meant that none stood out from the others. The town felt like a puzzle that had come apart and had never quite been put back together.

We got to the quayside as the sun was setting out at sea. Larger than Pag's dock, Komiža's quayside was fairly active with locals and tourists. Old men in ironed shirts and tank tops were chatting on a bench, and a woman selling wine and bottled capers was talking with her neighbours. Kids were tossing a ball on a wooden platform attached to the imposing *Kaštel*. In the harbour were a few excursion vessels, sail boats and dories, but no big fishing trawlers that hinted at Komiža's venerable fishing history.

The quayside is the most important part of social life in Komiža. Especially in the evenings, locals come to the quay and saunter along the bollards, chat, or just sit on the stone walls to watch life go by. The custom of an evening stroll in Croatia's island towns has no equivalent in the peasant villages to the north. Here, in Komiža, the quay has been the site of countless pageants, tombolas, rallies, brass band parades, and colourful wedding parties with songs and flowers and coins tossed at the newlyweds. The pastry shops along the quay sell custard, candied apples, ice cream. Funeral processions file darkly past.

FIGURE 20. The town of Komiža, island of Vis, 2013

Long-time resident, Jakša Fiamengo, had other memories of the quayside, memories from the Yugoslav years: "The deliberations before sailing, the greetings at the fishermen's return, enquiries who had escaped [in the 1950s and early '60s] and left his *leut* in an Italian port, the grief of Komiža when the military killed Jozo Pulenta in the night when he tried to escape to Italy with his crew. . . . The fishermen's nights with fish stew bubbling on the boats and fish exuding deliciously smelling smoke on the sacrificial fires [of the boats] along the quayside on St. Mikula's day, for the salvation of all boats at sea."[11] From the promenade, locals always looked out to the sea expecting news from abroad, waiting for the world to arrive at their shores, the next boat, the next event, the newest disruption to the tiresome repetition of their days. Waiting was a part of the experience of the quayside, as it was on islands everywhere.[12]

Joe and I walked to the end of the quay and around the corner, where we came to a pebbled beach right off the street. The smell of garlic and fish wafted out of a restaurant that had flung wide its second-storey windows. I took a swim in the evening light. I swam for ten minutes, then floated back to shore. The wet pebbles had a golden sheen, tinkling and crackling when I ran them through my fingers. Joe, who was sitting on the wall just taking in this new place, probably feeling the same thing I was—that it was good to be here—observed as I came up and sat down, "You see, Lucas made a big mistake not coming." He was referring to his grandson, who hadn't wanted to come to Croatia that summer. "This water, this water you can't find in Canada. He would be. . . ." He searched for the right phrase.

"In heaven," I finished the sentence for him.

"In heaven."

11 Jakša Fiamengo, "The Metropolis of Croatian Fishermen," in *The Island of Vis*, translated by Janko Paravić (Zagreb: Fabra 2004): 40–46.
12 See Predrag Matvejević, *Mediterranean: A Cultural Landscape*, translated by Michael Henry Heim (Berkeley: University of California Press, 1999), 17.

Then I got my things together and we walked back down the side streets to the harbour to find a restaurant. This decision at the end of a day of travelling was never a simple matter for us since we either couldn't agree on a place or couldn't combine the right price of meals with the right price of beer. The deciding factor almost always was the price of beer. "Look here," Joe said, pointing to a menu that was sitting on a table of one restaurant, "Ožujsko is twenty-five kuna here, and over there it's only fifteen. What do you think? No way," and he snapped the menu shut. The difference was around two dollars, but it seemed more in kuna (at that time, one Canadian dollar got you 5.3 kuna). The waiter, who had been standing by the open door of the restaurant, had just started to walk across the terrace to serve us, but stopped short when we left.

Walking back and forth on the quay some more, Joe pointed to one of the restaurants. "Look there, see the cats. All of them waiting by the tables for a snack. You feed one of them once and they never forget. Best is to give them nothing. Otherwise you have a problem, a serious problem."

Eventually we settled on a place for a meal, with Ožujsko, as people passed by on the quay and music played and cats nearby waited for a handout. I ordered *lignje risotto*, squid in a dark garlic sauce on rice. Joe had a grilled sea bass with olive oil, parsley, and garlic. We ate for a while in silence. I ordered more beer. When there was a lull in the music and the voices of customers around us, I could hear the sea softly clapping against the flanks of the quay. Then the noise picked up again and I lost the sea sound. I noticed a visitor beside our table. A scrawny cat a shade darker than caramel. "We have a guest," I said. Joe cast his eyes down and said, "Well, what do you want?" Then he stuck his fork into his last piece of fish and, after a covert glance around, dropped it onto the ground. The cat pounced on it and slipped away with it to some quiet corner. "You see how grateful he is," Joe said. We sat there longer, then we walked back up the knobbly stone street to our place.

The next day outside our cottage we spoke to our host, Srećko, who sat down with us this time. He wore a newly ironed short-sleeved shirt and pants, held up by the same suspenders. He was a serious, strait-laced man who had been born in Komiža in 1941 and had lived his entire life on Vis.

"I did go to Split once," he told us, "when I was sick, but never anywhere else."

"Have you gone to any other island?"

"No, I never saw the other islands. I saw them on the tele-vision, of course. But I didn't feel the need to go there. Why would I go when I have everything here?"

"How did you get around?"

"I walked. I still walk."

"You didn't have a car?"

"Never drove a car. School was close, just over here; work over there. I walked."

I asked him how much of his own island he had seen. "I have been to Vis, obviously, and other villages, but not all of them. There is much of the island I do not know. But I know Komiža."

"Sure, Komiža is home."

"That's right, home."

I didn't know if his lack of curiosity was the reason for not travelling or whether as an islander he inevitably lived in his own corner, his own island. It was the sort of insularity and lack of curiosity that reminded me of Štefek and Mila in Srebrnjak. They too lived on an island of sorts, except theirs wasn't surrounded by water.

Srećko told us he had eight years of regular schooling, one year in army school, and two years of political school. Later Joe said he meant a Yugoslav communist school. I wondered what they learned there, and he said, "What do you think? How to be a good communist!"

In broad brushstrokes, Srećko painted us a picture of his life after those years. He worked as a bartender in the only

hotel in town. Eventually, he built his own house, having lived with his parents and his four brothers his entire life. He tended his land and traded his produce for food in the lean years of Vis' isolation. "We were never poor; there was always enough to eat." His orchards and vineyard made him comparatively well off. Such were his connections with the establishment, and so big was his vineyard, that the local military commander in the 1980s ordered his soldiers to help harvest his grapes. "At that time, I had 18,000 litres of wine," he told us.

But not everyone chose to live on Vis. Around three and a half thousand residents of the island emigrated to America before and after the Second World War. Many left for California, Australia, and France. San Pedro, California, became the destination of choice, and an entire community of fishermen grew there, another Komiža in the new world. This was partly due to the skill, foresight, and courage of one man. At the turn of the twentieth century, a fisherman from Biševo, the little island off Komiža, had had enough of the hard life on land and at sea and decided to make a go of it in America.

FIGURE 21. Srećko Božanić at his home in Komiža, 2013

Martin Bogdanović, so the local story goes, "broke his hoe while digging in his vineyard. He was faced with a dilemma—fix the hoe or go to America? He decided to throw the hoe into the sea and leave for the States. He had just served his term in the Austrian navy and could freely leave his homeland."[13] This turned out to be a momentous decision. He became a successful fisherman in San Pedro. In 1914, he bought the San Pedro Fish Company, which sold fresh fish, and in 1917 with three partners and ten thousand dollars he built a small fish factory that became known internationally as Star Kist Food. The factory really grew during World War II because of the increased demand for canned goods.

Srećko told us that the fishing industry on Vis had declined in recent years. Fish numbers were down, and only one cannery operated periodically. Other crops on Vis were also in decline, like the flat leathery pods of carob trees whose beans were ground into flour that was exported as far off as South Africa, or used as a substitute for coffee and cocoa, or distilled into brandy.

By now it was early afternoon. Joe and I said goodbye to Srećko and went to explore the other side of the island. The narrow road took us past the huge thirteenth-century Benedictine monastery of Saint Nicholas known as *Mušter*, then over the southwestern shoulder of the island. When I saw no one travelling down, I drove in the left lane to avoid the horrifying drop off the right side. There were places to stop for a view, and when I got out to take some pictures, I felt the heavy fullness of the summer sun as it hit the exposed flank of western Vis. I could hear the loud stridulation of bugs in the dry grass and saw in the hazy blue of the sea the island of Biševo.

About five nautical miles from Komiža, dark green and seemingly close enough to reach by swimming, Biševo could

---

13 Joško Božanić, "Number One in the World," in *The Island of Vis*, translated by Janko Paravić (Zagreb: Fabra, 2004): 131.

be visited on "the line," a sea passage that had been operating since 1935, usually in the form of a small white boat. A Slovenian writer long acquainted with the island, Mate Dolenc, described the island's differing shapes and moods when viewed from Komiža: "Biševo lies in the sea like a dog, asleep with its head between its front paws, with a lighthouse at its rump. Sometimes it seems to be swimming and moving. And sometimes, when it gets dark and the scirocco is on the rampage, it almost disappears. And then after the bora, it comes so close to Komiža and you have the impression that you could step on it from the *riva* [waterfront]."[14] A few dozen people lived on the island during the summer, and just a handful over the winter. There were no hotels or cars, so the only way of getting around was by foot, donkey, or boat.[15]

I turned the last bend, crested the mountain, and began the descent. Along the road on our left was a barbed-wire fence made of concrete posts that curled at the top like candy canes. The fence had once sealed off the Yugoslav military's compound. The small road that turned left took us to our next stop, Tito's Cave, where Josip Broz himself had allegedly holed up during the Second World War when Vis became a garrison base for the Yugoslav National Liberation Army and Navy.

---

14 Mate Dolenc, "The Island of Wine and Submarine Caves," in *The Island of Vis*, trans. Janko Paravić (Zagreb: Fabra, 2004), 84.

15 The life to be found on the island itself has its simple beauties, but the main attraction of Biševo, for tourists anyway, is the "Blue Grotto" or *Modra špilja*, a cave on the eastern side of the island. It measures around 30 metres in length and 18 metres high, with a small opening for boats or swimmers to pass through. The opening was blasted out in 1884 on the advice of Austrian painter, Eugen von Ransonnet-Villez, who used to dive into the cave through a narrow fissure that was situated about two metres above the sea. Now, with the opening widened by the blast, the sun at its zenith reflects off the sea floor and shines an iridescent blue light around the cave's vault and through the water, giving visitors the feeling of floating in outer space.

The road to the cave was narrow, steep, and devoid of traffic. I parked and began the climb up wide stairs, following the red arrows painted on the rocks. It was hot and lizards by the hundreds skittered off the steps as I approached. When I finally got to the top, I saw a stone tablet embedded in a rock wall that read, "Here Comrade Tito stayed and worked in 1944 at the time when Vis was the headquarters for the political and military leadership of the People's Liberation War." From what I'd heard, the cave had been large enough to function as a hall and dining room, with a nook for Tito's Alsatian, Tigger. But what I found was much smaller, hardly bigger than a living room, marked everywhere on the ceilings and walls with black spots. A loud drone from hundreds of wasps or flies—I didn't stay long enough to check—issued menacingly from the cave.

On the way down, 290 steps by my count, I wondered how true these descriptions of the cave were. How reasonable was it for Tito to come here at all when he was already on an isolated island and could have stayed in some village instead?

When I got back to the car, Joe was waiting on a wall in the shade. He wasn't about to climb 290 steps to see a cave where Josip Broz or any communist had spent time. When I told him how many steps I'd counted on the way down he said, "So I was smart and you were not."

I drove up to the end of the road. We had come to Mt. Hum, the highest point on the island. I climbed a rocky footpath that led up to the chapel of Sveti Duh (literally, Saint Soul). From here I could see the orange roofs of Komiža and far out in the hazy blue the outlying island of Svetac, fourteen nautical miles west of Vis. Farther out, visible only in my imagination, was the tall rocky island of Palagruža, the island most distant from Croatia's mainland, halfway to the Italian coast, and alleged to be the final resting place of Diomedes, King of Argos.

The wooden door of the chapel was unlocked and inside, hanging from a nail in the white-washed wall, were a few rosaries. I looked back out at the wide expanse of blue sea and sky. This was the farthest I'd travelled from the mainland in Croatia's Adriatic region. It was the farthest south I'd travelled on this journey. I was a long way from Newfoundland where I lived, from the sublime landscape there, a long way from those drizzly grey days in the spring and the colossal mounds of blackening snow. I was in a different world than the valley from where I began this journey. And I was far from all the pressure of work. My wife and children were back there doing their thing.

I wasn't experiencing anything new in the history of journeys to southern Europe (a region often depicted in travel writing associated with the Grand Tour). Describing the Bay of Naples in her *Diary of an Ennuyée* (1826), Anna Jameson places the sea and its feeling of unbounded infinitude in implicit contrast to the "vapoury atmosphere" that she knows: "To stand upon my balcony, looking out upon the sunshine, and the glorious bay; the blue sea, and the pure skies—and to feel that indefinite sensation of excitement, that *superflu de vie*, quickening every pulse and thrilling through every nerve, is a pleasure peculiar to this climate, where the mere consciousness of existence is happiness enough. Then evening comes on, lighted by a moon and starry heavens, whose softness, richness, and splendour are not to be conceived by those who have lived always in the vapoury atmosphere of England." [16]

On Vis and on the other islands of Croatia, especially from summits like Sveti Duh, I had a similar experience of a "quickening pulse" and liberation from constraining bonds when I looked over the vast space of blue. The sea that was all around me, the contours of the coast of Vis and other islands nearby, the massive ceiling of the sky, blue like the sea, all of it added to the special "islandness" of the moment.

---

16 Anna Brownell Jameson, *Diary of an Ennuyée*, new edition (London: Henry Colborn, 1826), 250. Quoted in Chloe Chard, *Pleasure and Guilt on the Grand Tour: Travel Writing and Imaginative Geography, 1600–1830* (Manchester: Manchester University Press, 1999), 188.

We drove into a flattish open area on the southern side of Vis, passing villages, vineyards, lavender fields and dusty olive orchards—the only ones I had seen on Vis so far (olive trees aren't native to Vis and were only introduced in the 1980s).

The people of this area, *pojori* in the local dialect, still fished and still worked the land, but as in other parts of Croatia, rural life was declining. Evidence of this was all around Vis. I came across an abandoned stone house, with a lane leading in from the main road made of the same rusty beige stone as the house. A derelict beige Renault 4, the same colour as the stones, was parked in the back between the house and barn. A green cloth hung in the passenger window as though someone had just recently needed shade on the drive home. The house was a double-storey, which likely meant that its first owners had been relatively rich and had probably kept their animals on the ground floor (if they had not built their barn yet) while they themselves lived upstairs.[17] The people who had owned this place were long gone, like thousands of others who had escaped during the "barbed wire" period of Yugoslavia, or had left earlier during the phylloxera blight. The village of Podšpilje had a population of 1,500 in the 1950s, but now only 150 people remained. The buildings were here, though. This house seemed to be saying, "My builders are gone, their voices, their songs, but I am still here, still strong." I wondered whether the builders' families, somewhere overseas, even knew this place existed, knew they owned property on Vis. Could enough time go by for a property like this to be forgotten?

I returned to the car.

"What took you so long?" Joe asked.

"Did you miss me?"

"Oh yeeesss, it was lonely!"

"I noticed you kept the car on the whole time. Didn't think of turning it off and maybe opening a window?"

---

17 I am indebted to Goran Vojković for this insight.

"No, not really. It's hot outside."

"Okay, how about a swim?"

"Sure, drive on."

By then it was well into the afternoon. The sun was past its peak, the heat sunk deep into the earth. We came to the settlement of Milna on the shores of a small cove. From the road, the shallow water near shore was a bright, intense turquoise as though it were lit by a lamp underneath, then it grew darker fifty metres out where a line of white buoys had been strung.

Joe cooled his feet in the water while I swam beyond the buoys. It was my habit to swim farther than I was supposed to, like my grandmother's brother Otto, who used to dive under the barriers of the harbour in the sea in Schleswig-Holstein, even though a side of me was more and more cautious and knew all the dangers.

Back on land again, as I was sitting on the dock, a man in a black Speedo came down from his white bungalow. Bald but handsome, like a slimmed-down Brando in the role of Colonel Kurtz, he talked to us for a while as he stood in the water. When he learned what we were doing in Croatia, he invited us to his patio. "Just go on ahead, I'll be right there," he said. Then he jumped into the water for a dip.

We sat at a table in the shade of an awning and a fig tree. A cat was stretched on the steps on a spot where the sun flickered unevenly through the leaves. The wind was up, ruffling the surface of the cove, and two sailboarders were tacking at speed out near the island. Back and forth they went, and just as I thought they were going to break free of the cove and sail out to open water, they swung around again.

When our host returned, he offered to make us a pitcher of lemonade. I smiled to myself when I imagined Joe's reaction because I knew he was expecting something else. "It was okay," he said later, "I was tirsty," mispronouncing the word as he always did. So we drank fresh lemonade and talked about Vis with our host, Miljenko Vojković, a retired coast guard captain,

FIGURE 22. Miljenko Vojković at his cottage in Milna, island of Vis, 2013

sixty-seven years old, who spent much of the year on Vis but still kept his place in Split.

"My father was born on Vis in 1920," he said. "When he was a boy, he was barefoot most of the year, even in winter, though he sometimes wore a sort of slippers. He got his first pair of shoes, leather ones, when he was twenty and was going into the army. Yes, so, those were different times, people were not rich, but Vis, the island, was more populated than now. There were 10,000 people on Vis a hundred years ago. Now there might be three and a half thousand."

In his father's day, fishing and viniculture were the main industries, the former practised mainly in Komiža, the latter in Vis, though as I had already seen, there was evidence of a robust wine-making practice around Komiža. "Donkeys and mules were used for work. Mules were bigger and stronger and were more expensive."

"And no tourism in those years?" I asked.

"Not really. Of course, some people came, but very few. But you know there is this story, you've reminded me, of a traveller to Vis more than a century past. He was an Austrian, surveying the islands. This was during the Austro-Hungarian occupation, and he was an "expert." He asked some old guy the name of a nearby island, and the old guy answered, '*Kurva*.' So the Austrian wrote it down just as he was told. *Kurva*. 'Whore.'"

Miljenko laughed at the story as though he had never heard it before. I tried to picture the exchange between the two men, and it assumed various versions in my mind, with different satirical possibilities, the superior prig of a colonial representative versus the wily, uneducated, resentful local, or maybe the other way around, the practical, reasonable man of science for whom maps were needed, and the bovine, insulated islander who didn't need a map to know what the neighbouring island was called or how to get there, and who gives a shit about the rest of the world.

"Besides Vis, what other islands have you seen?" I asked.

"All of them. My job took me everywhere. I could go on a long time about them. Susak, the island of sand, with big steep dunes and sand beaches and canes, the only such island in Croatia. I saw the Kornati archipelago in northern Dalmatia—from the Italian, *Isole Incoronate*, 'Crowned Islands,' islands with no trees, white, like necklaces in the blue water. I have smelled the scent of herbs blowing from the islands when I sailed by. People from Murter, Sali and elsewhere raised sheep on the Kornati. When there was a drought in 2007, the sheep started to drink from the sea when the water ran out and they all died. The names of the Kornati islands are sometimes funny: Babina Guzica ("Grandma's Ass"), Kurba Vela ("Large Whore"). South of Korčula, there is the island of Lastovo. It is the second most remote inhabited island from the mainland, after Vis. In the main town, Lastovo, the chimneys look like minarets, though the Turks didn't settle there. Lastovo has a carnival, the Poklad, which is held every year before Ash Wednesday. The legend about it is interesting; five centuries ago when Catalan pirates sent a messenger to Lastovo ordering them to surrender, the Lastavans armed themselves instead. They prayed to Sveti Jure (St. George) to protect them. Their prayers were answered because a powerful storm sank the pirates' fleet. The citizens of Lastovo sat the messenger on a donkey and rode him through town and then burned him to death. For centuries, a straw puppet, the *poklad*, has replaced the messenger."

Miljenko the sailor was quite different from Srećko, the communist. Miljenko was a traveller, a man of the sea, while

Srećko was a landlubber, even though he lived on an island. Miljenko, from what I could gather, was an energetic person. By his own account he was also a reasonable and logical one, scientific in mentality. He told us he didn't care much about debate. When he listened to politicians wrangling about some issue or other, he got pissed off. "*Daj šuti*," he said, slapping the air (and the politicians) with the back of his hand, "Keep quiet."

We sat there a while longer, chatting some more. The windsurfers were coming back now, and it was time for my father and me to go. But I felt like staying on. Miljenko told us he lived here on Vis much of the year, when the tourists had finally gone and it was quiet and he could still enjoy the sea. He continued to swim and fish. Who knows, maybe one day we would return to see Vis in that different mood. Already I had a twinge of regret for having to leave. I had already formed a nostalgic longing for Komiža, for the vineyards of the pojori countryside, for the whole island.

I looked at Joe.

"Time to go?" I asked.

"Time to go."

A Slower Tempo
✝ Hvar

When next I went to Srebrnjak, my fourteen-year-old son Lucas travelled with me. He hadn't wanted to go the summer before. "What am I supposed to do there?" he'd asked. "It's gonna be boring. Walking in the hills? Yeah right, dad." This year I told him, "Deda Joe has a .22. Ivek Mikek, the guy he escaped with from Yugoslavia in 1963 gave him one. It belonged to his brother. You can maybe use it—there are pheasants." As an afterthought, another temptation, I said, "Oh yeah, and you can have crispy boar like Asterix and Obelix, or crispy pig. Down there in Rakov Potok, they roast them all day long." He said, "Okay, but there's only two things I want to go to Croatia for: the roast pig and the .22. Don't think I'm gonna have any fun besides that."

We flew into Frankfurt and drove south through Bavaria, then the next day through the Austrian Alps, as I had the year before. It was a pleasure for me to see everything through the eyes of my son. That was a difference in my trip this time. I looked at every experience through him: The incredible vistas, the cars that tore past us on the Autobahn, the schnitzel, the life-sized crucifix with the painted blood in the room where we had our continental breakfast in a village on the Chiemsee.

Many of his activities in Srebrnjak were layered with my own over the years, so that when I observed him, I saw myself too. When he went for a run on top of the hill, I thought of myself back in 1987 doing the same. When he did planks or sprints in the cool evenings on the street, or push-ups, it reminded me of my own discipline and training when I used to run fartlek intervals way back when. Joe said, "He doesn't need to do this. I have plenty of stone he can move to get strong. Plentyyyyy!" Not everything Lucas did reminded me of myself, though. With the sticks and thirty pucks we'd brought, he shot half an hour every day at a makeshift net my father had built. The plastic on it tore through right away and I ended up running in the grass with a pail to collect the pucks. But when Lucas rode the dirt jumper I'd bought him and drove on the road and around the place, launching jumps over the flower bed on the son-in-law's land next door, which caused the man to have a fit, I revisited my own bike rides down the Srebrnjak road, relived my own departures, returns and adventures. When Lucas sat at the table for a meal with guests who didn't know English, sat there a little stiffly and not saying anything, I remembered myself in similar shoes all those years ago. They were strange for me, these double experiences; haunting but pleasurable too.

I didn't feel old that summer, didn't feel the pressing reality of time having gone by. Every day brought certain duties, so I was satisfied living within the structure that came with them. And yet there were times, especially when I started to write, when a stark awareness of the passage of time stung me. When I thought how far in the past the past actually was. Where be your gibes now? Your gambols? Your songs? Your flashes of merriment that were wont to set the table on a roar? That's when I felt like stomping harder on the pedals and tearing down the road faster. . . .

In that frame of mind, to push back the years a little and to test myself under the heft of a full summer sun, I went on a long bike ride from Srebrnjak into the Samobor Hills.

I also wanted to experience the country up close again. I hadn't been on a bike here in years. I missed exploring the villages, seeing the little things you don't see driving in a car.

What I found was that with every kilometre as I rode deeper into rural Croatia, I was also ticking back the years, back to an earlier time.

The hot day was filled with summer life—birdsong on all sides, a weedwhacker snarling in a field somewhere, sparrows in swarms looking for bits of gravel on the paved roads and clearing out of the way at the last second when I rode through.

The severe hill from the main road to Marija Magdalena gave me a great view of the sharp peak in the blue distance, the medieval ruins of Okić and, beyond that, the Žumberak hills and Slovenia. That was the direction in which I was riding. A memory of walking to the chapel with Tea returned to me; standing together inside the church and making those pretend vows; then our walk down the Srerbrnjak road, hand in hand. I felt myself transported back into the moment again, and yet, as I stood there leaning on my bike, swimming in the nice feeling of it all, my memory seemed too beautiful to be real, like a vision in which I had been dreamed into life by someone else.

But the physical world was solid and just as I remembered it. A vineyard near the chapel clung to the steep sides of the next valley, Bušićka. Empty plastic bottles, as always, had been cut open and placed on the pointed poles so they would rattle when the wind blew, to scare off birds. A wooden wine *klet* with a concrete terrace and wooden benches was at the top of the vineyard. (Later, I learned that the klet belonged to none other than the son of Kata Deak, the sister of Draga Husta, and that a few years later it would be burned down in retribution by the son of the woman with whom he was alleged to have had an affair.)

Two roads diverged and I took the one of rough clay and stones into Bušićka. Images returned to me of pitchforking hay onto a wagon here twenty-five years ago. Slavko and John Deery. The ride back to the barn on top of the swaying wagon. The view from on high. No worries, no thoughts about the future. Those were the days!

Driving my bike west into the afternoon sun, a farrow of white clouds piled above the hills, I came across three roads that gave me the exact same option—climb or go back—and I began to climb. When I saw a hale elderly guy walking towards a café, I shouted to him, "These hills have grown since last year," to which he answered with a wave, "And the bar always seems farther!"

A sharp, brutal incline followed. From there I turned left towards the village of Galgovo, then I passed Nataša's bar where some fans were gathering before a soccer game, then the fire hall, inside which men were socializing, and then on past a concrete soccer court where kids were booting around a ball.

Beyond that lay the country. Head-high corn, a wide field of nodding daisies and buttercups and chamomile, a churring of insects, swallows skimming the surface of the land. Sliding off on a westerly current was the same brown hawk as always. A linden tree stood on one side of the road across from a tiny chapel called Sveto Trojstvo, which had a bell and was inscribed with "M. Ž. 1907," possibly the name of the builder.

I rode deeper into the Samobor Hills. The new Croatia hadn't made many inroads here. In the village of Konščica, perched on a very steep hill, stood a sagging wooden house in which someone still lived, and an old barn covered by faded blue plaster with two cows inside.

Following a sharp descent through thick woods where the temperature dropped pleasantly, I hit the killer hill to Klake and, right by the village sign, as I bent over my bike to recuperate, I met a seventy-nine-year-old villager called Vilim Razum on a red Zetor tractor by his vineyard. "I used to be a master glassblower at the crystal factory in Rude," he told me, "and now I just mess around here." Vili, as he was called, told me he had various grapes—graševina ("*Welschriesling*"), muscat, and *kardinal* (a red variety)—and said he usually produced a few hundred litres of wine every fall. Vili liked to talk and had a long memory. When I explained who my family was, to my astonishment he remembered my grandmother's husband, Husta.

After our conversation, I rode the twisting lane through the rest of Klake, a tidy village of newly façaded and well-kept wooden houses, then I turned left towards Okić through more thick woods where there are wild boar, foxes, and deer. The castle at the top is the blue peak I had always seen on those walks around Srebrnjak.

Onward to Kotari as the candent globe of the sun began to sink towards the big western hills. I was soaking wet and tired, but I pedalled on. I wasn't rushing, wasn't trying to test myself any longer, or trying get to the end of my journey faster. I knew the hills had beaten me, there were no two ways about it, so I just settled down into a steady rhythm and enjoyed the ride.

I passed plum orchards, the plums already covering the ground, waiting to be collected; I saw freshly cut firewood stacked everywhere and, at the top of the village, in the open space where there was a bus stop, the view of mountainous forest-covered hills rolling on to the west like waves pushed to the shore by ceaseless tides. I felt the same quickening of pulse as I had on top of Vis, the feeling of being on the summit of an island surrounded by the sea. In deep, gorge-like valleys covered by deciduous trees were more villages of the kind I had already seen. A large peak to the west was called Japetić where there was a mountaineering hut and restaurant. From there you could see the highest point in the Žumberak on the border with Slovenia, Sveta Gera, and then on a clear day the highest mountain in the Julian Alps and all of the former Yugoslavia, Triglav.

Samobor was an orange pointillistic shimmer in the distance below. I headed there, passing more small villages, and arrived finally at Samobor's main square, where I collapsed into a chair and had a beer and watched the crowds. I was soaking wet, and my legs were fried. I would have happily stayed there the rest of the evening, had more beer, and watched the people go by. I thought of calling Joe to pick me up. But I still had the last leg home and I felt I should find it inside me to finish the ride up under my own power . . . the final ride back home through flatland and wide fields and a long straightaway near Kerestinec where fireflies in the growing dusk danced on the edge of the road.

FIGURE 23. Stacked wood in Kotari

That summer, Joe, Lucas, and I drove south to the island of Hvar. Joe was in a good mood. He was looking forward to our trip because his grandson had finally come to Croatia. We three had never gone on a trip together before. And so, on the ferry, he had a few celebratory drinks, periodically taking long slugs of his white wine from a plastic container he kept in a cooler. I cut up sausage and cheese. Joe took more slugs of wine and then, all of a sudden, began to remark on the legs of the women sitting across from him. In English, but a little too loudly, he said, "Those are great legs; you're not going to find much better legs, let me tell you, when they point up at the sky!" Lucas shook his head and laughed. I passed Joe a piece of cheese. "Here, eat this. This will keep your mouth shut."

We sailed into the town of Stari Grad through a long fjord as the sun beat down on the dark blue glittery sea. The hills around were thickly covered by dark pines, and here and there was a house strung off a thin gravel road.

When I first sailed to Hvar back in May 1996, the scene had been different. It was night, and a wildfire on the northern tip of the island lit the night air, varnishing the black surface of the sea. Among only four or five passengers on the ferry, I had stood on deck taking in the scene. A heavy cool wind had begun to blow.

At dawn the next morning, the wind rattled the wooden shutters of the room I had rented. The shutters banged insistently for a while and kept me awake, so finally I threw them open and looked over the faded terracotta roofs of Stari Grad through the pale morning light. Founded by the Greeks in 385 BCE, at which time it was called Pharos, Stari Grad ("Old Town") felt like a small Dalmatian town typical of those island settlements secondary in importance and size to the main ones which, on this island, is Hvar.

It was a cool Sunday morning, the northern bura still driving through. Stari Grad's cobbled streets were empty.

The shutters were sealed tight, and church bells, shredded by the wind, tolled somewhere in the heart of the town, ringing parishioners to mass. I walked around with no particular purpose, and with plenty of time.

At the harbour, there was more life as some locals on their small fishing dories busied themselves with their nets or stood around by their tour boats talking or having a coffee at a café. I was the only tourist. I walked out of town on the empty promenade that went along one side of the narrow bay. The wind was roughening the sea, which was blue-black and looked cold.

When I returned later, I came across some elderly men playing bocce on a dirt court in a side street. There were five or six of them standing over the balls discussing something. I thought I knew these guys! They looked just like the men I'd seen on other islands. I remembered the ones on Korčula, like these, wearing the same white undershirts, short-sleeved collared shirts, shorts, sandals. I remember that the guys on Korčula weren't discussing something; what they were doing was arguing; they were arguing over the position of the balls, whether a dark metal ball or its white counterpart was closer to the jack.

A tall skinny guy with a thatch of white hair who seemed to represent the black ball said to a short guy with bandy legs and round glasses, "It's obvious if you look."

"I am looking and nothing is obvious to me."

"That's because you are looking at it from the wrong angle, come over here and you will see better," the tall man said.

"Why would I go over there when it is the same as over here? Didn't you study geometry in school?" the little guy answered.

"I studied it same as you! Listen, perfesser, take that bicycle off your nose, maybe that will help you see better."

"I know how you did in school, so don't talk to me. And I can see fine, don't you worry."

"Then just go get the stick and we will measure the balls," the tall one said.

"We've gone over this before," the little guy answered, he was starting to move around on his short bandy legs in agitation, "the stick is bent and is not to be trusted. We need a new stick."

The tall man threw up his hands. "Like this we will go on forever. I say we start again."

The little guy eyed him a moment, then answered, "Why would we start again when it is obvious."

"I am looking and nothing is obvious to me," the tall one said. And so it went on . . .

Returning to the centre of Stari Grad on that trip in 1996, I happened across Tvrdalj, the mansion of Renaissance poet Petar Hektorović (1487–1572). A grey stone structure that Hektorović began in 1514 as a stronghold against attacks by Turkish pirates, its quiet halls and courtyards, sunlight filtering here and there, gave me the feeling of a secure and peaceful retreat. I saw a dark pool of slow-moving fish, other objects that portray traditional Hvar life like a pan for hot coals to warm a bed, and various solemn inscriptions in Latin carved in stone throughout, "Alas, the days flow by like waves and do not return."

The guide to Tvrdalj at the time, a young man with a boyishly handsome face and brown hair, Tomislav Alaupović, led me to the sun-dappled garden courtyard of mint plants, fig and olive trees, and exotic Mediterranean flora. Here, where Hektorović himself tended his garden, one can find a fitting homology for his poetic energies, his sixteenth-century poem *Fishing and Fishermen's Conversation*.[18] Often called the first realist poem in Croatian literature, it is a travel narrative in

18 The poem is dated 4 January 1556 but most likely concerns events from the previous summer.

the form of an epistle to Hektorović's cousin, relating the journey of the nobleman poet and two fishermen from Stari Grad
to Šolta and back. Wrote Hektorović:

> There are so many people who appear simple,
> Poor and ill-clad and yet have plenty.
> For such people are possessed of
> Reason and sound judgement which are their clothes;
> So virtue dwelleth in them secretly
> Like the gold covered by earth:
> We think them no more able than the sea slug,
> Yet when they speak, they speak like sages . . .
> And here I said to them: "As you see,
> My brothers, all has been as we planned.
> Well have we voyaged across the deep sea
> And well returned to our island home.
> You have sung and recited plentifully
> And your many talents deserve every praise.
> Where are the knights now of whom you told,
> The dukes and princes whom you mentioned?
> They are no longer of this earth,
> Nor scarcely are their names known;
> No more than dreams I'd say, as those of other men . . .
> Time hath borne them away on its silent flow." [19]

After visiting the mansion, I spent a few hours exploring
the rest of Stari Grad. Later I returned to the house where I
had rented a room. The patriarch of the place greeted me and
invited me for a meal. He led me into their small dining room
where the table was already set. His wife served us sardines
and squid fried in garlic and olive oil, and he brought out a
carafe of his red wine. We talked while his wife stood by the

---

19 Petar Hektorović, *Fishing and Fishermen's Conversation*, translated by
   E. D. Goy, *British-Croatia Review* 15 (January 1979): 13–45; lines 1473–1527.

door to the kitchen listening. He was a short, black-haired man with a face like a browned pork chop. At first he was cheerful. For example, he told me, pointing at the sardines, that "a fish has to swim three times: in the sea, in oil and in wine." But his mood soon changed. "You know," he said, "this is not a good time for us in Dalmatia. Everything has changed since the war. No one comes now. You are the first this season. Stari Grad is empty. Probably the ferry was almost empty. . . Am I right? Yes, I thought so. Before, when it was the high season, the Germans came, thousands of them. One day things will get better again, but it will take time, maybe years. The Germans might not come again. Look at our house, we added to it for the tourists, but now they are not coming." Neither he nor his wife held a job; only their daughter worked, it seemed.

The daughter, the waitress who had called her brother from the bar the night before when I'd inquired about accommodation, arrived while we were still at the table. She was motioned over by her father with a discreet nod of his head, not apparently meant for my eyes. Her face was masked by white foundation and her lips painted dark red—a Gothic look. She had just finished another shift. As I talked with the father, she was silent, but I noticed her watching me, her big placid dark eyes looking out from her white vampire face. She told me something about her plans for university, which I can't remember, then she said, "You know, my friends and I are going out tonight. Maybe you would like to come. We have plans for tomorrow night. And the rest of the week. Every night. The night is the best time."

I was evasive. "I planned to go to Hvar early tomorrow," I said, which was not a lie, "but I might be able to come back. I'll see." I was trying to untangle the reasons behind her invitation. Her parents watched me, waiting for my answer. I could feel the daughter's big black eyes on me. The next morning, I took my things and was on the bus to Hvar.

All this went through my mind as Lucas, Joe and I docked. It was a different time in Dalmatia's history. The dearth of tourists the man had mentioned had ended. There were no Germans, but our ferry had been packed with Croatians, Poles, Czechs, and Italians who drove off in their luxury cars to the other side of the island and to the town of Hvar.

We, however, drove to Stari Grad. I expected a different town this time, but I found it almost as sleepy as it was on my first visit. At the round head of the harbour, roughly the same number of boats were moored. No yachts or fancy ships. A kid sitting on a boat with a long pole poked leisurely at a hub cap on the floor of the harbour and, under the dark surface of the motionless water, dark green fish like the ones in the pool at Tvrdalj swam lazily. Only a few tourists wandered through the streets.

We walked around looking for a restaurant. As usual, Joe and I argued about which one we were going to choose, but this time we had the added complication of a fourteen-year-old who had ideas of his own. "Can we have pizza? I want pizza," he said. "You can't have pizza," I answered. "You had pizza last night; you can't just eat pizza. And drink pop. A pork chop with fries, and some *ajvar* on the side, that's the thing. With milk. You're supposed to be training. And that's what your mother would want."

He looked at me. "Who cares? Mom's not here, dad."

Joe, who had been listening, said, "I don't know what he's going to eat, that's your business, but I know one thing for sure." He waited.

"What's that," I asked.

"I'm the pensioner and you're the rich man, a professor, so you're going to be paying, ha-ha," and he let go that cackle of his.

"Funny," I said, and he began to laugh even harder, his face turning purple. I looked inside my wallet and saw I didn't have any kuna; there was a twenty Austrian Schilling bill I kept as

a souvenir for some reason, and a credit card, neither of which would be any use at these restaurants. Otherwise my wallet was empty. "Okay, we're all set," I said, "let's go eat!"

We decided on a restaurant not far from the riva that served pork chops with fries and ajvar, among other things, and were waited on by a young woman, the daughter of the owner. She was a tall, beautiful girl with a beautiful mouth and black hair past her shoulders. She was studying law in Split but worked here with her father over the summer.

I told her that Stari Grad was a nice town, that it must be a good place to live.

"Well, yes," she answered in English, "it is very good town in summer, when there is life, and there are people. But, you know, it is not so good in winter. I have been here in winter; it was not good. It was so depressing. It was totally dead; there were almost no people. No young people. You could walk through streets and hardly see anyone. They are all gone to Split to study. And then it is windy and cold. The bura, you know of the bura?"

FIGURE 24: Stari Grad, island of Hvar

"Yes," I said.

"The bura it is not nice wind!"

I thought of the howling winter winds in Newfoundland that drive snow horizontally across my yard and whistle around the bungalow, creaking the aluminum siding and tearing strips of snow from the eight-foot-high mountains along the streets.

"I understand," I said.

"Yes, so anyway, Stari Grad is much nicer now."

"You no longer stay here in the winters?"

"No, and my father shuts the restaurant and goes to Split."

"Do many islanders do that now?" I wondered.

"Some, yes, though there are elderly ones who were born on Hvar and never leave. And not just elderly ones. They don't know anything except this. Imagine not knowing anything else!"

"If you don't know it you don't miss it."

"Well I would miss it."

"You would also miss your own island."

"It is not my island. We came here after the war, from Bosnia. But I understand your point. I was young when we came, and so I think Hvar is a kind of home. For my father it is more complicated." Her father joined the conversation, talking in vague terms about his own origins and reasons for coming to Hvar, then getting more heated when he remembered those days, rehashing familiar grievances against the Serbs for their part in altering his life forever.

It was time to go. I opened my wallet, tilting it towards Joe who was sitting next to me. "Look at that, would you," I said, "I must've used my last kuna paying for gas. You're gonna have to cover this, sorry to say." Joe was in a good mood after chatting with the restaurant owner, plus the man was watching, so he laughed with pretend ruefulness, and reached for his wallet without hesitating.

We said goodbye and went to our apartment. I left my father and my son there and went in search of my only contact, Tomislav, the former tour guide at Hektorović's mansion. When I met him again, as he was holding court with some local guys, I thought he looked like a different person. He was still handsome, his light brown hair thinning, but the polite almost diffident young man had been replaced by a larger, grander one. He was bigger around the middle, but the real change was inside, evident in his easy demeanour, in his stance, the calm gaze of self-possession. He knew who he was, where he belonged, and nothing was going to rattle him. He looked me over, and I wasn't totally sure he liked what he saw. But he was friendly, shaking my hand, "So you've come back to Stari Grad! I guess you like our island. And what's not to like!" I told him I was here with my father and son. "Ah," he said, "the three generations travelling together!"

The next morning when I went to town to shop for bread and a newspaper, in a rush walking briskly past the same café where I had seen Tomislav yesterday, I heard him yell out at me, "Hey, what's the rush? *Pomalo*. Slow down, man, slow down. You're moving too fast. Never move too fast!" I lamely held up my loaf of bread as a sort of explanation, slowed my steps and carried on towards the apartment. "You're in Dalmatia," I heard him call out, "never go too fast!" Someone in the pastry shop laughed through the open window. I was embarrassed a little and my first instinct was to walk faster, to get away more quickly, but I corrected myself. I had heard this idea of slowness before about Dalmatia, usually in the context of a contemptuous remark by those in the northern parts of the country, that the people here are lazy, like *tovari* who have to be prodded, lashed, to get to work. In fact, the word for donkey, *tovar*, has become pejorative slang for "Dalmatian." Probably this stereotype has its origins in the reluctance of Dalmatians to work during the afternoons, but everyone knows what working in the sweltering heat is like, including those in northern Croatia where this stereotype apparently originates. The Dalmatian fjaka, which I've mentioned before, came back to me now with Tomislav's advice; he was encouraging a fjaka-inspired ethos in living life generally, not just how quickly or slowly I should move, at what pace I should walk down the street with a loaf of bread, or how much energy I should use after a hefty meal on a hot summer afternoon, but my mode of being and my frame of mind when I get out of bed in the morning and carry myself throughout the day and just in general exist. The frenetic hurry of the rat race would seem foreign to the Dalmatian character.

On this day, in this island town, on a summer vacation, I thought that Tomislav was right. What were another few minutes going to matter? Would my father and son starve if I brought this loaf of bread five minutes later? I remembered my first stay in Stari Grad, the slow unhurried walk around town, the tempo of my whole stay on the island. Much had gone on in the meantime, more responsibilities and pressure, and like a billion other people I had lost that tempo. As I walked back to the apartment with deliberate slowness, I thought that with this visit to Hvar maybe I could rediscover the right pace. Maybe Hvar could be the start of something new. Something new, something old.

We drove to the southern side of the island on a well-paved road that took us out of Stari Grad into the flat breadbasket country of vineyards and gardens (a UNESCO Heritage site due to its ancient plots of land dating to the Greek period). In the distance was the mountainous ridge of the island still blued by morning shade.

After some turns through rocky hills, we came to the tunnel at Pitva. The green traffic light told us to go, so we drove in slowly. A kilometre and a half long, the tunnel resembled other barebone ones built by the military in the former Yugoslavia. It was a bumpy, narrow one-laner through a low, pitch-black passage that sweated with condensation. The ceiling looked like it had been hacked out with pickaxes by some guys who had had too much to drink. The opening at the far end was a pinprick of light, and there were two parking spaces in case cars met head-to-head, which happened when the locals didn't bother obeying the traffic light. Caches of wine, it was said, had been stored in the tunnel because of its cool temperature. "What if we get stuck or there's an accident or something? What then?" I joked. "Then you're going to have to walk, sonny boy, all the way to the end," Joe answered, firing off that cackle of his, which he did when he enjoyed sticking it to me.

Out the other side and into the day again, we zigzagged over wide sloping hills, through craggy fields of white-grey stones spotted with evergreen maquis and wizened trees. Eventually we came to Sveta Nedjelja.

We parked and walked straight ahead for a view of the sea. We had stepped onto a four-metre-high islet called Veli Kamik attached to Hvar itself by a walkway. A tree grew in the middle of it, and some stairs led down to a concrete dock that had been built for mooring small boats.

I knew this place! I had come here on my first trip to Hvar, in 1996. Without any forethought, I had jumped joyfully into the sea. Waves slapped and gurgled against the high cliffs of the cove, and I had swum out to open sea, where the water roughened, and where I turned back to look at the island, the white shoulder of the mountain behind. Only when I slid back up to the dock did I realize I couldn't get out. There was no ladder, and the water was too low for me to pull myself up. No one was around. No tourists, no one to help me. This was 1996, and the coast was deserted. My excitement about being one of the only visitors to the coast at a unique moment in its history changed to panic. Even if someone spied me from afar, they would have thought I was waving, not drowning. Now, the idea of striking out to sea and swimming around the islet and along the coast in search of a place to get out was a scary one. In that moment, I didn't know how close the harbour was. I decided to stay and find a way out, treading water, checking along the edge of the dock and the islet's slippery flanks for some foothold, something to grip. I was angry with myself for having jumped into the water without thinking. Finally, when I was sure I would have to swim for it, I noticed a thin, ragged rope the colour of the stone, like a muskrat's tail, attached to a pike that someone had nailed there, probably having gone through what I had, and I pulled myself out.

Lucas and Joe stayed on the islet while I went to Sveta Nedjelja. A village of around 140 people, called Sveta Nedilja in the local *čakavski* dialect, it sits part way up the mountain of Sveti Nikola. This is the highest point on the island. Savage grey-white cliffs amphitheatre the village and the vineyards on the slopes below, shielding them against direct blasts from the northern wind. I parked and walked uphill to the vineyards, through olive orchards and past copses of Aleppo pines. Tall cypresses, like minarets, stood here and there. The sun had come out; now, in the late afternoon, the large bowl of the valley under the mountain was packed with dozens of vineyards that formed a carpet of light green when you looked at them from a distance. Some of the vines grew low to the ground, and many were thick and twisted, like arthritic trunks of old trees. A hothouse aroma rose from the warm ground.

I saw a man in a vineyard off the road. As he walked down the low row of vines, he bent over and clipped the odd leaf, then moved on, looking closely at his grapes. He wore a baseball cap and a blue T-shirt, and his thin arms and hands were as gnarled as the branches of old vines. He had come to look at his vineyard. "There's not much to do here now," he said, "I let the sun do the work." In the north, in the hills around Zagreb where it rains more often, bunch rot can be a problem; here less so. On Hvar, the grapes soak up the heat and are cooled by winds that come across the mountain or sweep up from the sea.

The man and I treaded between rows of vines up to a stone wall where another vineyard grew on a higher terrace, then we came back down again. Dry, grey-brown karst soil crunched under our feet. He swung his right arm over the vineyards around us and turned his grey watery eyes to me. "This is Plavac Mali. Take a look; you can see." The grapes were small blue nodules packed closely together. The name of the grapes was appropriate—*plavac*, from *plavo* or "blue," and *mali* meaning "small." "This vineyard was planted by my grandfather in the 1920s, but there are older ones too, and newer. New vineyards are business. Mine is not so much business, just my own business, ha-ha." He went on, "Plavac Mali is a very old grape. The scientists say it took good qualities of the parents—one is Dobričić from island Šolta, and the other is Crljenak." He meant Crljenak kaštelanski, a variety of Dalmatian origin, also known as Tribidrag, neither of which is widespread any longer.

"The Americans call Crljenak Zinfandel. You know of Zinfandel, famous American wine, but it really is old Dalmatian type."[20]

---

[20] The genetic identification of Crljenak and Zinfandel is an interesting story that began in the 1950s. Croatian-born vintner Miljenko "Mike" Grgich (Grgić) had suspected from the moment he had arrived in California in the 1950s that Zinfandel was Plavac Mali and eventually approached scientists at the University of California, Davis, about that possibility. In an email interview, grape geneticist Carole Meredith wrote that "I was interested in finding the European home of Zinfandel, which has been established and important in California for well over 100 years but, unlike all the other major wine grapes, was not associated with any particular European region." So when Croatian researchers contacted her in 1997 for help in studying and preserving their own varieties of wine grapes. she "jumped at the chance because I (and others) had long suspected that Croatia might be the home of Zinfandel." Their subsequent research "showed that Zinfandel is indeed a Croatian variety . . . but also that many of the indigenous Croatian grape varieties are closely related to Zinfandel" (Carole Meredith, pers. comm., 28 January 2015). Crljenak is also genetically identical to Primitivo, introduced to Puglia (the easternmost tip, or "heel," of Italy) in the eighteenth century.

"I didn't know that, but I've heard of Plavac Mali. It must be good," I said.

"You never tried? Come, I show you."

He led me out of the vineyard and down the gravel road to his house. In his cellar, he took out two drinking glasses from a cupboard, went to a steel barrel, opened the spout, and filled them. He knocked his glass against mine and said "Živjeli!" The wine was ruby red, transparent like a stained-glass window. It filled my mouth with a touch of sunshine followed by a drier taste of stony earth, if it were possible to turn the minerals of the ground into smooth liquid. I felt I had travelled from the bright hot summer sky down to the dry karst earth on which I had walked just earlier. I liked his Plavac, and I didn't have to lie when I said, "It's good."

He told me more about his vineyard, said that last fall's harvest yielded 500 litres of red wine. Some of his wine he sold to restaurants in Hvar, the rest he drank himself. He wasn't interested in making a large profit. "What do I care," he said, "I sell what I sell, and that's it. Look around, I have everything I need. I have enough to live. What more does a man need? Those young guys," and he named the owner of a large local winery, "those guys they export their wine all the way to Australia, can you believe it?"

As he talked, his thin brown hands lay on the table between us. When he leaned forward, I could see pouches under his watery eyes, accentuated by the light from the bulb above, the surface of his face like brown onion skin pages in a worn-out anthology. His grey hair curled tight and thick like steel wool. At one point he got up, went to the cupboard, and returned to his chair, covering his mouth with his hands, and worked at something between his teeth. After a bit he said, "All my life I have made this wine, and before that when I was a boy, I helped my parents collect the grapes during the *berba*. Our whole village was out here harvesting; you could hear them talk and joke. There was singing; the valley was full of singing.

Songs from the far side of the valley. And you know what, we worked together, helped each other in those days. And if you had trouble with someone over the year, you let it go during the berba." He stopped and finished what was left in his glass. I asked him whether life was better in the old days. "Better, maybe, maybe better, now it's everyone for himself. That was not a thought before." I asked whether this was due to the attitudes in the former Yugoslavia. "No, my son, that was just life on Hvar. My life on Hvar."

With that, I said goodbye, left his cellar and walked down to my car. I came to the harbour, and the restaurant, a newish building built out of stone, where Joe and Lucas were waiting for me. My father had a glass of red wine, my son a pearling bottle of Coke. I had been gone a while.

"Where have you been?" Lucas asked.

"Were you worried?" I answered.

"Oh sure," Joe said, "that's all we've been thinking about." And they laughed.

The narrow road from Stari Grad to the main city of Hvar climbs in hard switchbacks across the mountainous island and descends sharply on the other side (where, if you take a left on a winding trail along the sea, you return eventually to Sveta Nedjelja). In 1996 I took the inland road from Stari Grad to Hvar on a bus driven by a big man who wrenched the steering wheel back and forth along the wicked turns. The doors and emergency hatches were open to let air blow through the bus. Along the way were forlorn houses, their shutters closed, roofs sinking, and people long gone. Some inhabited settlements and small stores appeared too. Below the road, in the valleys, amid pines, olive and carob trees, rock piles and walls, were small gardens, vineyards and swaying fields of lavender.

Now the new road from Stari Grad to Hvar passes through a modern tunnel and leads with modern efficiency to the island's main town. Built on a hill beside the sea, Hvar is a town of stairs overlooking the open sea and an archipelago of eleven small, forested islands ringed with white stone, known as the *Pakleni otoci* ("Hell's Islands"). The houses piled on top of each other seem to tumble towards the rectangular harbour. In this elegant town you can find the largest square in Dalmatia, one of the oldest theatres still standing in Europe (1612), and numerous palaces such as the one that once belonged to Hanibal Lucić (1485–1553), author of the first secular drama in Croatian. A UNESCO World Heritage site, Hvar replaced Stari Grad as the island's capital in the thirteenth century, and wherever one looks it projects an image of a refined, cultured and happening resort.

We arrived in the outskirts, which were more ragged and unkempt than the showy centre of town. While Joe chose to stay in the courtyard of the apartment we had rented, chatting with the owners and drinking more wine, Lucas and I walked to the riva by ourselves.

We passed through an opening onto the quayside, which was lined by palm trees, and where young women with long legs held signs to draw customers' attention to the restaurants. Beautiful, ample girls in miniskirts sashayed by us, their perfumes noticeable as they swept past. I pointed out a few Lucas' age and suggested he go talk to them. He had been walking beside me, looking stiffly ahead, but alert and wired. "Yeah right, Dad," he said. "You'll be sorry one day, sonny boy," I answered. "Just keep walking, Dad." We kept walking. Big sleek yachts like sharks were lined up perpendicularly to the promenade, flying Bahamian, British, American, and Italian flags. One white-haired owner, chic like Richard Branson, was wearing a pressed white shirt whose crisp folds I could make out from a distance as though the shirt had just been removed from its package. Another owner sat back on a lounge chair with some ladies in airy summer dresses and pumps who were drinking white wine from fluted glasses. But amid this elegance, an Italian in a blue Speedo, just off a newly arrived yacht, staggered back and forth in front of his boat singing, beer can in hand, then rolled onto his back and shouted something con brio as his buddies laughed from the deck. Although it was early in the evening, and early in the season, Hvar was already showing its character as a popular party destination.

We came to the head of the harbour, where we could have continued along the promenade and out of town, but dusk was settling dark blue around us, so we went back. On return walks like this my eyes always hit upon new sights, or are drawn back to the same ones I'd seen before—the cream-coloured columns of elegant buildings, the polished stone slabs on which I was walking that glistened when the lights came on, the palms along the riva, a yellow lantern hanging above a street, a ceramic pot with an oleander, flowering white, a row of green shutters. On a backstreet in 1996 I had seen an old fisherman in his white undershirt and shorts sitting on a pail repairing a white fishing net that hung from his balcony like a huge bridal train. Over the next few days, through gaps in the lanes, I saw the sea from high above and motorboats zippering white trails behind them like jets across the sky and smelled the aromas of sea breezes blowing through canted corridors.

We saw him, a short young man, T-shirt over his head to protect himself from a hot morning sun, dandering along towards us on the highway two kilometres outside Hvar. We had parked our car on the road and were about to descend a rocky path to a beach far below. The Irishman, who said he was from Dublin, told us he'd been partying on a yacht in Hvar's harbour the night before, and when things had quieted down early in the morning he'd gone to sleep below deck.

"Next thing I knew," he told us, "we were out at sea in the morning sailing God knows where. All my things, my car, clothes, were back in Hvar." The English owner hadn't known he was aboard and had left bright and early for some other port.

"He wouldn't box the compass, so I told him to drop me as close to shore as he dared. Then I swam for it, shoes and all." As an afterthought he added, "I had to leave my cell phone behind."

Now he was here, at ten in the morning, pleasantly strolling towards Hvar, the whips of panic just a memory.

"How far is it to town?" he asked.

"Not two kilometres," I answered.

"Right then," pulling his shirt over his head. "Goodbye."

"Bye," we answered. And off he went, a free man, a proud swimmer striking out for a new destiny.

The steep trail down to the beach was a long one over rocks, so Joe balked at coming with us. The Adriatic was to our right, a smell of herbs around us. There were broadleaved cacti, eucalypti, and wild grass. A few years ago, there used to be a forest of big pines here, slanting against the steep slopes, and cicadas clacking furiously, but the trees had been cut down so instead there was an orchard of young olive trees and cicadas somewhere in a glade to our left, much more muted. We could see down to a small cove. Some century-old stone houses, once a fishing hamlet, lay at the head of a beach of white pebbles, and on one side of the bay, on a piece of land jutting out to sea, was a much larger stone house, formerly belonging to the wealthiest family of the hamlet.

We walked onto the beach. Its roundish stones were already warmed by morning sun. Only a few people were here, and no one was in the water. We put our things under a pine tree and, while I sat watching, Lucas hobbled over the stones and walked into the water up to his chest. Then he dove in. He disappeared for five or six seconds, then popped up three metres away, then went under again. Over and over he repeated his dives. When I joined him, he pointed out fish near the bottom, silver-blue, much smaller than the sea bass we had tried to catch barehanded off Cribbon's Rock in Antigonish, Nova Scotia. I watched him dive deep for a stone, a shell, crouch on the sea floor and rocket up to breach the sea's surface. When I treaded water, I felt hot sunshine on my head, saw a bright sheen on the water like a polish made of light. I floated on my back, not moving, ears under water, hearing a soft underwater roar. I lay there blocking out everything, trying to stay in the moment and enjoying the slow tempo on Hvar as the words of advice returned to me: "Take it slow, man, you've been moving much too fast, pomalo, pomalo . . ."

I went back to my towel and dried off. As I waited for Lucas to finish, I noticed an elderly man appear from one of the small stone houses. Wiry and bowlegged, he wore a red and grey flannel shirt and grey pants, as though it were a cold December day, and he stepped unsteadily outside his gate and looked out to sea. Then he went inside. Later, when Lucas was drying off, the old man came out again. Maybe he had come to check on the guy who had emerged from his big house, a big man with a thatch of white hair and no shirt. He was on his concrete dock about fifty metres away, untangling some fishing nets beside a dory. Possibly he'd been out that morning and was tidying up. Or maybe the old man wasn't interested in him at all. A few steps from the guy with the nets was a slim woman in a bikini bottom and no top, tanned all over, helping him. They were focussed on their jobs, didn't speak to each other, or take any notice of the old man who had been watching.

I went over to the old man's house to talk with him. A blue tin sign that read *sobe* was nailed to a wall at the entry to his yard. Marigolds in pots sat on a low wall and grapes grew along a wire trellis on the right. The ground was made of paving stones and packed earth. He met me coming in as he was going out. Up close he resembled the winemaker in Sveta Nedjelja, but this man's hair was white, a little wispy and wild from the wind, and contrasted sharply with the brown skin of his face. His nose reminded me of Jimmy Durante's and the skin on his face was tight to his cheeks, healthy-looking, though I thought he was unmistakably in his seventies.

He talked in a quiet, high voice, telling me he was born elsewhere on the island—he named a village; I forget which one—but that his father had bought this property years ago and had passed it on to him. His wife, the woman going in and out of the open door in the yard behind him, was not his first wife, but his second wife, and she was from Split.

"Have you talked to that man there? he asked me and pointed at the man working on the fishing nets.

"No," I answered.

"Do not speak with him. He is a bad man, an evil man."

"Oh," I said.

"Yes, yes, he said once he would kill me." He whispered so I could hardly hear him, and his eyes opened wider.

"He and his brother, they wanted to have a café here, right here on shore. I told them I did not want it. I knew all would change here. People, hundreds of people would come. There would be garbage, and there would be noise. They would play music," he whispered angrily as he leaned forward.

"Yes, there would definitely be music," I said.

"One day they were bringing supplies by boat. Two men were carrying a barrel of wine onto the beach. I ran into the water and pushed them, and the barrel fell into the water. I tried to turn over their boat, but I could not. The man there swore he would kill me. He was very angry, and I was afraid. I walked back to my home. Now we never talk. We have not talked all these years."

"When did this happen?"

"In 1998."

The café never went ahead. He looked over my shoulder once more, then turned back to his house. His story was at an end. He led me to a table in his yard that stood in the shade against a wall of his house. Lucas came over; the wife served us juice, and the old man, relaxed now in his chair in his yard, told us about his life. He said he lived on Hvar all year. They rented out their extra room to tourists from time to time. He and his wife went shopping for groceries once a week. He was eighty-one and she was seventy-three, and they carried their groceries down the winding path from the road above.

The old man asked me if I would like to try his wine. I declined. Before we left, his last words to me were these, "Do not talk to him, he is a bad man, an evil man."

Lucas and I climbed the path to the car as the noon sun pounded down. We had taken a last dip and now, water dripping off our heads, we dried off in the wind and sun. I was in no rush. I took my time picking my way over the stone path so I wouldn't heat up again. I looked out at the Adriatic, which was dark and shining, a white sail a kilometre out, not moving, like a splotch of white in an impressionistic painting. Cicadas strummed in the trees behind me, growing fainter the higher I climbed, the stronger the wind got near the summit, sending their signals out to sea. Long grass bent back and forth with the breezes. My hair was already drying, and when I got to the top it was almost dry. I took a last look over the sea, at the sun glittering white on the dark blue waves, and I thought that if I could fly, I would fly from these cliffs and across the water and become part of the white light on the sea.

Yugonostalgia

Joe and I were sitting at the table on the front terrace of his house. Plump feathery clouds perched lazily on the hill across from us; the hawk was up there doing his usual thing. I could see the barn below us and the massive walnut tree that blocked off a view of the old house in which Štefek and Mila had lived.

"They're all gone now," I remarked.

"Life doesn't go on forever—what do you think?"

"I wasn't just talking about the swallows," I said. He had told me that the son-in-law, the one who had stolen the apple I'd saved for my grandmother back in 1977, had boarded up the hole in the barn through which the swallows had used to fly when the big sliding door was shut. And now that the ditch had been covered over and the pipes put in to transport water from Samobor, there was no water for the swallows. They had moved on.

"I was talking about the people."

"I know that."

"There's only Jana left."

"That's right."

"Of the people here who knew you when you were a kid, I meant."

"That's right."

"What do you feel about that?"

He thought for a moment. "Nothing. What else is supposed to happen?"

He wasn't sentimental about it. Unlike me, he didn't concern himself with thoughts of the waning number of people who knew him as a boy, his ever-growing isolation from his own childhood.

"It's a different country now, a different life," I said. "Do you think it's better?"

He stopped to think. "Sure, it's better, but how much better I don't know."

Croatia's entry into the European Union in 2013 had had some positive consequences, like funds for urban renewal projects, subsidies for farmers, and duty-free exports into the European market. On the other hand, there was high unemployment and emigration of educated youth to other E.U. states. Right now, people were proud to be Croatian, and there was no going back to the old Yugoslav days. Yet somehow there had been a rise in Yugonostalgia.

For example, in 2017 there had been blowback among some politicians, journalists and ordinary Croatians about a decision by the cities of Karlovac and Zagreb to rename streets and squares still dedicated to former president Tito, thirty-seven years after his death and twenty-six years after Croatia declared its independence from Yugoslavia.

"I guess some people think Yugoslavia wasn't so bad," I said.

"Not so bad. But not so good," he laughed.

"Those politicians who call themselves anti-fascists say fascism is on the rise."

He smiled that wicked smile of his. "In this country, they think anyone against communism is bad, is a fascist. They call themselves anti-fascists because they don't want to use the word 'communist' anymore."

"Why did it take so long to change the street names?" I asked.

"There were old communists in power before, so no one made a change," said Joe, "even at the beginning of the new Croatia. These politicians said they were nationalists then, but they didn't want to say goodbye to Tito. It's finally time to get rid of him."

There was more going on in Croatia than a revival or suppression of Tito in the interests of political advantage. Not everyone I knew in northern Croatia felt things were better now than they were in Yugoslavia. It wasn't Tito some people missed but a way of life gone for good. And that didn't only mean lost job security, or the dwindling of farm life, that old family vineyards were disappearing, like the one Miško had decided to cut down because he was too old to do the work any longer, and his son was unwilling to carry on, the vineyard my grandfather and his brothers had planted at the start of the twentieth century. When I thought of the brothers digging the long trenches, imagining that all their work would come to something, when I considered that my grandfather hardly had a chance to enjoy the fruits of his labour before his life was cut short in the war, before he even met his own son, his brother dying soon after of tuberculosis, it bothered me that Miško had had that pleasure instead, although yes, I know, he did work for decades. It wasn't like he was gifted something, and I know the vines were not all the same, yet I felt Miško had been disloyal to them when he cut down the vineyard.

What people missed about Yugoslavia was also the camaraderie and collective spirit that was no more. My thoughts went back to my early years in Yugoslavia, the work people did in the fields together, the conversations and jokes and gossip, the post-haying get-togethers with gemišt, all the collective labour over a lifetime, the closeness of neighbours. My wife recalled some of her own experiences, "When I was a little girl, women would pluck the slaughtered chickens to make pillows and blankets. They spread the feathers on the table and separated the fluff from the quills and the women sang while they worked. I can hear them now. It's a fond memory of my childhood."

Emblematic of this tightness between the people in Yugoslavia coming to an end was the strange falling out between Jana's husband Dragec and Milivoj, their big neighbour in Dol. Something happened that even the neighbours I spoke to over the years didn't know about, a secret acrimony that festered for fifteen years and caused the two men never to speak again. I wanted to ask Dragec what had happened but always thought better of it. In his last years he was bedridden. Hip-replacement surgery and wounds on his legs that never healed, which Jana had to treat every day, kept him in the bedroom downstairs. His mind was still lively, though. He could tell stories, crack jokes, knew all about the politics and sports of the day. If I came to visit, he allowed himself a glass of wine and let loose on some issue or other and enjoyed a good laugh. So having a mind that worked was a godsend from a certain point of view. However, for Dragec, having a sharp mind was a double-edged sword because he knew all too well his hopeless situation. When I think back to him and Milivoj after a session of haying, sitting at the table by the outdoor kitchen and drinking wine and talking, the friendship still intact, the friendly wine flowing, I know it was a better time. Veliki dečec! Big Boy.

Joe and I were working one morning on the slate tiles of the driveway, which drew the attention of a neighbour, who came over to chat. Milovan was a sixty-year-old interpreter by profession who told us he'd just finished translating the most recent Spider Man flick for the Croatian cinemas. Joe and I had been discussing the street names again.

"You have it wrong," Milovan told me in English, "This feeling for the past has nothing to do with Yugoslavia versus Croatia. It has everything to do with the economy. The average person is worse off than before. The economy is 1,000% worse.

You just cannot get ahead today. Simply cannot. Employment among youth is high. Maybe it is improving, I grant you that, but you are faced with the choice of living here with a doubtful future or leaving. That is what the new Croatia is."

Thinking more about how good Yugoslavia was, Milovan went on, "There were freedoms. You could travel out of the country whenever you wished, for example. That is not any different than today."

"Hold on," Joe said, "I couldn't just leave the country in the 1960s. There was not this freedom that you say. I had to escape to get out!"

"Well, you were young and hadn't done your military service. But by the late '60s it was different for the public. Things had loosened up."

Generally, he was right, but not all parts of the former country were so liberated. The island of Vis was a military island closed to all outside traffic until 1989. And at least into the 1960s if residents wanted to leave, they had to do so secretly. Many tried to escape by sea in the night and many were caught; some were killed.

Yugonostalgics tended to overlook other obvious problems with their former country. Unless you were a bigshot communist insider, striking it rich was impossible. There were jobs, but the pay wasn't great and there was never really enough work; factory labourers often finished their quota after only six hours, then would sit around playing cards for the remaining two. Service across the board was rude and slow. Saleswomen in state-owned department stores preferred smoking and talking to serving customers. At the border you could run into trouble if you ran across the wrong guard. My father with his Canadian passport and Croatian last name drew the ire of the Serbian-born police who didn't like it that he was a Yugoslav emigrant; they made him wait and then rifled through all his suitcases. A similar thing happened to me travelling by train from Paris to Zagreb in 1989, when my passport was taken at the Yugoslav border in Slovenia, and I was asked to step out into the cold winter day and wait outside the control office, inside which I could see the passports piled together and waiting beside the guard's still steaming coffee.

My wife said that when she was a young girl in the early 1980s there were *nestašice*. During these shortages, stores would run out of things like sugar or coffee, and when news spread of an incoming supply somewhere, everyone would swarm to the location. Around 1982, there were blackouts every third night from eight until eleven.

Nevertheless, there were plenty of pro-Yugoslav communists still around. Miško had been one. I remember the small golden bas-relief of Tito in the hallway of his house. On the same day we had spoken to Milovan, Miško stopped by to borrow my father's sit-down lawnmower, and we had a chat. "I was a member of the Party, yes, for a few years, but then I quit when the fees became too high and I wasn't getting anything out of it." He spoke a little sheepishly as thought he were embarrassed. Asked whether he thought about life back then, he said, "Some things were definitely better. Everyone had work, that was the big thing." But when I wondered whether he would like to go back, he said flatly, "Not a chance. The Serbs controlled too much." This was a familiar refrain in Croatia today. There might be nostalgia for Yugoslavia, but it didn't run deep enough to become a full-blown movement.

Joe and I sat outside a while longer, then later in the evening went upstairs to watch the semi-final between England and Croatia. It was the year of Croatia's run to the World Cup Finals. People's spirit and pride of country were high. A guy down the street in Srebrnjak had started off the tournament by grilling pork chops before Croatia's first game, then had gone gastronomically bigger with each successive win, marking the occasion of the semi-final by roasting a whole pig! Croatian flags hung off balconies and were wrapped around the mirrors of cars and families gathered in their yards for barbecues hours before each match.

The game turned out to be oddly analogous to Croatia's uneven progress out of the gate after independence. England had the advantage 1–0 after the first half, but increasingly Croatia improved. First Ivan Perišić stabbed in a cross with his left foot to equalize and then Mario Mandžukić slipped into the box during extra time and slid home the winner. We went crazy. I leaped out of my chair and screamed. Joe spilled his wine. When I pulled open the slider and ran out onto the back terrace, I could see fireworks and flares above the hills and hear gunfire somewhere in Molvice. Pop-pop-pop-pop. A rumble like thunder seemed to shake the ground and I sent a barbaric yawp over the rooftops of the valley.

FIGURE 25. Evening in Postira, island of Brač

Brač Revisited

The year 2020 will always be remembered for the COVID-19 pandemic, but in Croatia it will also be remembered for two earthquakes, one in March, the other in December. After the final tremors ended in March, snow suddenly began to fall in Zagreb. It was an eerie sight in Croatia's normally temperate spring. To people under lockdown, who were facing a pandemic for the first time, the earthquake, then the snow, seemed to presage the end of the world.

For me, because COVID-19 locked me down in western Newfoundland where I lived, preventing me from leaving the island as I did every year. I found myself journeying more and more with my other selves to far away places, the antipodes of my regular pandemic life. These included my return trip to the island of Brač, the island I first visited in 1977, the first island I ever saw. My return there became both a memory and a series of wish images of what could be again.

When I thought of my first visit to Brač and remembered the boy of long ago, I had a strange feeling of him joining me now. The kid who ran around Srebrnjak in his lederhosen, who dreamed of being one of the Fellowship of the Ring and of having adventures, who liked to read and draw, sensitive to things, who had no special ambition and hadn't done anything yet and had no idea or worry about where his life was going to go—that kid was with me again. He couldn't see me, but I could see him. I remembered the stifling drive south on the Magistrala back in 1977, my grandmother complaining about the open windows; I recalled the intense light of the sun and blue of the sea, the contrast between green Srebrnjak and the arid coast. I thought too of famous Zlatni Rat beach, which had underwhelmed me back then. I wondered what impression it would leave on me this time.

Going to Brač was another reprieve from everything back there, from the chaos of Split's ferry docks, from the whole world I was leaving behind again. At sea, the city looked different immediately. Cleaner, less chaotic. I saw the panorama of the old town—the cathedral of Sveti Duje (Saint Domnius), the line of palm trees and the southern façade of the palace of Roman emperor Diocletian that once was washed by the Adriatic, its white limestone harvested from a quarry on Brač—and then the modern city itself, its grey Lego-block high-rises toothily sticking out of the karst rock. Split's suburbs and other settlements stretched south along the mainland shore like beads on a string. Somewhere was Bačvice beach, where hip trendsetting Splićani spend leisure time and where the game of picigin originated. Behind the city is the Mosor mountain range, part of the tail end of the Dinaric Alps. At the base is a green carpet of vegetation, then above that the rock itself. Right now, with the sun shining brightly the stone was whitish grey, but at other times the stone changed hue. In the late afternoon, Mosor was coppery orange, and the shadows of clouds passed across its face.

After a fifty-minute crossing, the ferry arrived in Supetar. I drove to my accommodation in Postira, a small pretty town on Brač's northern coast. The narrow road wound parallel with the sea through a forest of tall Aleppo pines that leaned to the water from years of the prevailing wind blowing off the island's upper slopes. Now in the early evening, the setting sun sent its last rays along the road, pushing my car's shadow ahead of me. Through gaps between the trees I could see the turquoise water near the shore.

When I arrived and stepped out of the car, I smelled the pines, the rosemary and sea water. It was a peaceful evening. People were coming home from a nearby beach as music from town drifted along the coast.

There was still time for a swim. I changed and went down to the sea and onto the brown rocks, from where I swam out into the channel as the sun set. Underwater, I could see thousands of tiny sardines moving casually in torpedo-shaped schools. From Split and the settlements along the coast, a few lights were starting to flicker orange. In the dusk, breaking the surface of the dark glassy water, I swam for a while as swallows skimmed the surface of the sea and flew on to Postira.

Afterwards, I went out for supper. The street below my apartment took me directly to Postira's old section. Hundreds of swallows swerved above the street and into gaps in the stone, or up on the rafters where they had their nests. The sky was filled with the swallows and their high-pitched cries.

The closer I came to the centre of town, the stronger the aroma of burning wood from an open fire at a restaurant. Its owner was standing over a stone slab where embers were burning. I watched him stick some sardines on a spit, then do the same with seven or eight other fish and lay the spit on two stones at the edge of the fire. On the grill were other skewers of meat and vegetables and some larger cutlets. You could walk from the street right into the restaurant or stand by the stove as he cooked, to decide whether you wanted to eat there. I asked him if those were pork *ražnjići*. "No," he said, "these kebabs are swordfish." The TV in the street said they had roast lamb. "We have no more today," he said. "You must come earlier. Come tomorrow at seven and there will be some. Any later I cannot promise." He stepped onto the street and pointed over a roof at the hills. "My pastures are up there, not five kilometres from here. Fresh lamb, organic, everything organic."

I ate at a restaurant down the street, sitting on a terrace with a view of the channel. The water was turning black and the mountains on the far side were already black. Bats fluttered around the streetlights where earlier there had been swallows.

The woman who served me was a Postira native and student of Croatian literature and culture at the University of Zagreb. She had lived all her life in Postira, but now she was gone most of the year. "I do not miss the island anymore," she told me in English, "I do not miss the winter here."

"But it's colder in Zagreb than on Brač. And there's snow."

"Yes, but it is change for me. And there is more life in Zagreb."

"I met someone in Stari Grad who told me she thought her town was depressing in the winter," I said.

"I do not know if that is right word. I think the islands are so sad in winter. Yes, sad is word I would choose."

"What do people do on Brač in the winter?"

"Life goes on. In Postira we have *Sardina*, sardine factory. I think it might be only one in Dalmatia. The factory employs many people on Brač. Some men fish for their families. But there are fewer fish. Some families have pastures and sheep, so I guess there is some work to do. But in winter tourists do not come; the towns are empty. You ask me what people do in winter. Well there is lot of boring time. Young people ask, 'Do I go now or stay another year?'"

She went back to work, and I sat a few minutes longer. A more sobering picture of island life had revealed itself again, hard to imagine on a fragrant warm evening like this one with tourists aplenty, music playing, people dancing and a view of the mainland across the channel where orange lights shone like fireflies.

Fifteen kilometres from Postira, on the island's north coast, lies the town of Pučišća. Many of the buildings in town, around the island, and throughout the world are built of stone from quarries in Pučišća and the surrounding area. In addition to Canada's Vimy Ridge Memorial and Diocletian's Palace, Dalmatia's Šibenik Cathedral is made of Brač limestone, which was also incorporated into both the Austrian Parliament building, in Vienna, and the Hungarian Parliament building, in Budapest, along with the Palazzo del Governo, or Governor's Palace, in Trieste, and many other stately buildings. So, wrote one commentator, "The people of Brač say that in the past fifty years more stone has been excavated than in the period from Diocletian times until the twentieth century. If all the shiploads of Brač stone exported around the world were put one after another, they would by far exceed the length of the Great Wall of China." [21]

In a Pučišća quarry, men operating jackhammers drilled at the white stone and white dust rose in the air and settled on their clothes and hair. Inside the stone mason school, young *škarpelini* in overalls and jumpsuits worked on blocks of stone with hammers and chisels, practising the deft art of carving. I saw rosettes, crosses, elaborate windows, bowls with variegated edges—all of white stone, reminding me of the lacework from the island of Pag. A former master at the school, Zdravko Matijašić, said, "A future stone carver must truly feel the soul of stone. He must have a feeling for its hardness, for the sound of it, he has to be able to hear when the stone calls to him, when it says 'yes' to him, and when it refuses him and says 'no.' And finally, the stone master must know how to read light in the depth of the rock and pull it out into the open." [22]

21 Josip Antić, "The Continuous Brač Wall," in *The Island of Brač*, translated by Mark Davies et al. (Zagreb: Fabro Press, 2006), 112.
22 Cited in Josip Antić, "The Continuous Brač Wall," in *The Island of Brač*, trans. Mark Davies et al. (Zagreb: Fabro Press, 2006), 112.

The road to Škrip took me uphill into the island's interior, past more old olive groves, rock walls and rock mounds than I'd seen on any island so far. From a distance, the country was wooded and dark green, the green of deep summer, striped with grey stone. Up close, I saw dense pockets of pines, mixed with the occasional oak, carob, almond and fig tree, and under-brush of myrtle, various junipers, and shrubs like Spanish broom, rosemary, and pomegranate. A bright sun outlined, scalpel-sharp, the grey Mosor mountains on the mainland. The road was good, wide, and paved with new blacktop as it approached the old village. In 1977, when I first came to Brač, inland roads had been gravel, which made the interior feel more desolate than it did now.

Škrip is the oldest settlement on the island. One of fifteen known prehistoric forts on Brač, its megalithic walls were probably built by the Illyrians with the intention of repulsing Greek incursions. The village sits on a hill, and the country falls away on all sides, rising again to the south.

When I stepped out of the car, I was swarmed by elderly ladies waiting for visitors like mosquitoes that rise from the grass. The first woman who approached me was tall, had short black hair combed to the side like a boy's, and wore black from top to bottom. A golden chain with a crucifix hung around her neck. "Good day, sir," she said, "I have wine, and *travarica*, olive oil and honey. You must try, sir, please come this way, over here, it is not very far, see just over here," and before I knew it, I was herded down some stairs to the back of her house and into her basement, a spacious room with ten-foot-high ceilings. The room was filled with the stuff of her working life and castoff things from another time. On the top of a table she had set up some bottles with their prices printed on slips of paper.

She ploughed straight through my reluctance, pouring red wine into a cup for me to taste and herb brandy in a bottle cap. "The wine is 30 kuna a litre, the travarica 70." That was around $5.50 and $13.00 Canadian respectively. "Here, you must try. Come here, don't be shy. You won't be disappointed. These are real homemade products from the island of Brač." Vanja Radojković was a widow of seventy-five who earned extra money from tourists during the summer to supplement her pension. She owned land behind her house where olives grew and where once sheep had grazed. "That stopped when my husband died," she told me. "We owned fifty sheep at one point. We had many hectares of land. I made

FIGURE 26. Vanja Radojković outside her home in Škrip, island of Brač

cheese we sold to tourists here and in Supetar. Now it is too much work, so I do not make cheese any longer."

"This wine is yours?"

"Yes, I have a vineyard," waving her hand out the open door. "It was cut back when my husband died."

"Do you do the work yourself?" I wondered.

"Yes, and my son helps me. For the berba there are neighbours too. He comes to see me every day. He lives on the coast, but he is here every day. That is fine with me. That way I can make sure he is not getting into trouble," she laughed.

I looked around her basement. A framed picture of Mary holding Jesus hung on one wall. There were some steel barrels along another, a pitchfork and shovel, a few shelves with glass demi-john bottles, and some dried squash gourds hanging from a nail. She noticed me eyeing them, picked them up and put them under her arm. "We used this to help us swim when we were children. Ten kuna a piece!"

I bought a bottle of wine, but not a gourd, and said goodbye. When I was on the street again, a second woman stepped in front of me. She was short, wore a blue ball cap, her white wispy hair in a bun, and carried a basket of lavender. Or, more exactly, sachets of lavender with the name "Brač" written in fine script and tied at the top with purple string. "Hello, young man," she began. "Here is something that smells sweet, something to remind you of our island. If you have a nice young wife, I am sure she will enjoy lavender from Brač." She held out one of the sachets. "Ten kuna each." If I could afford a bottle of wine, I had to buy a sachet of lavender.

I got out my wallet and gave her the money, took the sachet, and smelled it. "Thank you," I said.

I was going to walk on when she touched my arm and said, "They are small; one is not really enough. Maybe you have a mother who would like lavender. You cannot forget about your mother. Here, take another. Take two."

I didn't really want two. One was enough for me. And I already had one. But when I looked down at her, a little talkative woman with white hair girlishly unkempt and holes in her smile where there should have been teeth, a woman who smiled at me good-naturedly, a little slyly, as though it were all a conspiracy in which we were on the same side, even though I was playing the role of the gullible tourist and she the wily local peddler, I caved in and bought another sachet.

"That's it," I said, "thank you. I have enough now, thank you. Goodbye." The first sachet I stashed in my camera bag, the second in my pocket. I kept the one in my pocket for several days until I noticed that the string had come undone and the lavender had spilled out. I kept it there for weeks to remind me of the old lady in Škrip.

Clearly, my encounters with these women showed what they were forced to do to keep themselves afloat, and perhaps was evidence of the reputation of Brač residents as tight-fisted. One scholar, however, has written in their defence, arguing that every "island is a world of restricted quantities. This knowledge instructs the islander to ration the goods that nature benevolently proffers to him or that he obtains from nature through his hard work. The Mainland, all too lightly, names this island rationing as stinginess."[23] Here is a joke I heard about the reputed stinginess of Brač's residents: an islander had published an obituary for his recently deceased wife in *Slobodna Dalmacija*, a paper printed over in Split. They called him up to inform him that for the same cost he could add three or four more words to the notice. They suggested he insert "She died peacefully" or something similar. After a moment of silence, the shrewd widower answered, "No, put 'Olive Oil for Sale.'"[24]

On the return to Postira, I drove on a twisting country road past stony sheep pastures and low walls of dry-stacked rock. It was a quiet evening, no cars were on the road, and most of the island's visitors were on the coast. I parked by a wire gate between stone walls and entered a pasture and closed the gate behind me. The wild grass beneath my feet was cropped; there were sheep droppings all around, and in front of me, throwing a wide shade, stood a tall holm oak from which hung a disc of salt. A broken-down moped with a plastic bag filled with

---

23 Joško Božanić, "Terra Marique," in *The Adriatic Archipelago Telling Tales*, translated by Stipe Grgas (Split: Hydrographic Institute of the Republic of Croatia, 2010), 122.

24 It is a joke that gets to the heart of the people and the history of the island. The olive trade, once critical to the economy, took a severe downturn in the 1870s because of islanders' decision to replace trees with vines. This decision had its logic at the time when phylloxera had invaded the vineyards of France and Italy, but not those on the Croatian coast, so that many Brač residents tried to exploit the rise in the price of wine. They cut down thousands of olive groves and planted vines in their place. A tragedy for the island of Brač then unfolded as the phylloxera blight infected its vineyards not long after. Many families were ruined. An exodus from the island followed. Thousands left for the United States, Australia, and South America. Many emigrants from Brač found their way to the saltpetre mining region of northern Chile and Tierra del Fuego in the glacial south.

shavings for a seat, leaned against the tree. And there they were, a flock of twenty sheep drinking from plastic water containers. They were surprised to see me, since I'd made no noise. They bleated once or twice, then when I stepped closer, they clattered up a pile of stones and skittered down the other side, bells clanging, echoing loudly against the surrounding stones.

I looked around the glade. Myrtle grew by the rock walls along with bay leaf and wild roses, and in the back part of the pasture were olive trees. I came across a *bunja*, a hut of stone with a conical vaulted roof. This type of ancient structure can be found throughout the Mediterranean, serving as a single-roomed home or as a way place for shepherds. This one was relatively new, more shelter than hut, with a triangular stone step sticking out of the wall to make it easier for the shepherd to access his door. The entry was low, and in the crawlspace was room enough for one person. Inside were seat cushions and a pair of old leather shoes. The shepherd might be the restaurant owner in Postira, or some local living in an interior village like Škrip, and he used this hut when he wanted to get out of the way of the bura or a rainstorm passing through.

I walked around the glade taking pictures. The sun was starting to set. The wind had left for somewhere else, so a peacefulness had come into the evening, like a friendly mood. A few last swallows swerved through the copper-gold air and the cicadas were quieting down. I made sure to close the gate behind me and went back to my car.

The next day I drove to Nerežišća. Built into the foothills of the island's highest mountain, Nerežišća was formerly the island's administrative centre but now has an atmosphere more like a village than a town. The grey-white Sveti Petar chapel in the main square, with its Romanesque and Gothic elements, resembles similar stone chapels on the island and throughout the Adriatic, and might have been forgettable were it not for a bonsai pine tree that grew miraculously through its semi-circular apse. Over a century old, the tree was small and scrawny, but tough. There, in an unlikely and inhospitable spot, it had somehow survived. To me it seemed a symbol of the islanders themselves.

After photographing the tree, I explored the narrow alleys of the old town. A nun I met stopped to talk to me outside the Baroque parish church. She had a round sunny face and a sunny demeanour. Sister Emilja Šimić was born in Livno, Bosnia-Herzegovina, but had put down roots on the island with the other nuns in the convent house. She said, "We are none of us spring chickens, but we have our duties and we are happy. Today is a beautiful day! Would you like to see the church? I will show you the church. Come, follow me this way."

Inside the cool, spacious church, near the front altar, another nun was polishing copper thuribles with a dish cloth. Sister Alberta Maslač was a tall woman with a handsome face, smooth skin, and gold-rimmed glasses. A different energy came from her. She spoke in elegant, long, and somewhat sententious sentences. She informed me about the history of her church, said it was constructed and designed by Ignacije Macanović and told me other details I've forgotten. She was knowledgeable and eloquent. I asked her whether she had studied at university.

"No, of course I have not; it was never in the plans for me."

"Who knows, if you had, what you could have gone on to be," I said.

"Well, it is interesting to think so," she answered.

I asked her what she enjoyed about her life here. She said, "You know, I think it is the work with the children that gives me most pleasure. Yes, I think that gives me the most joy." She was looking at me through her gold-rimmed glasses, observing, thinking about something. There was a silence in which she put the final polishing touches on the thurible.

"You know," she said, "there is something in you that I see.

It is a light you have inside which God has given you, and anyone who looks more closely will see. He who seeks shall find. You are good in your spirit, you are not arrogant, and you are looking for the truth."

"Well," I said, "thank you."

"It is not me you have to thank."

I didn't know what else to say. She put the thurible on the pew, and we shook hands and said goodbye. A kind of warmth, a feeling I hadn't had for a while, went through me as I got in the car and began the drive to the top of the island. I was feeling Sister Alberta's words as I drove up into the deep woods of big black pines with the sun peering down into the gaps, the cathedral-high spaces, and onto the brown pine-needle floor. A rinsed cloudless blue sky was visible above the jagged treetops, then it opened wide at the summit. I got out of the car, stepped across white limestone crags, and saw the view.

This is the highest peak on the Croatian islands. Vidova Gora. To the east the wide wooded land sloped down majestically to the sea. To my right, the west, the island of Šolta lay in a white-blue haze, and to the south, across a narrow channel, was the northern, sparsely habited coastline of Hvar. I stood on a rock that projected outwards into the abyss. On the right was the famous Zlatni Rat beach, the beach I hadn't seen in all these years, and which had left me disappointed the first time. It pointed thinly out into the turquoise shallows of the sea where, farther out, yachts in the circumambient dark blue floated, not moving, like white flecks on a canvas. White plumes of motorboats tore up the dark channel behind. What looked like parachutists pulled by boats hung motionless in the air. A warm wind blew across the summit and down to the sea, and the white-hot sun was poised above Hvar, radiating upon the southern coast of Brač and on the beach. I stood there for a while taking in the view. The smell of pines came on the wind and cicadas clacked furiously from the trees. I hadn't seen any pictures of Zlatni Rat from Vidova

Gora before this moment, even though there are hundreds online, as I now know, but the view was a thrilling one for me, not only because it was a beautiful one but because it was verification of the aesthetic value of Zlatni Rat itself, that its fame was deserved, and that I was participating in its fame just by looking down at it from on high, from where it could really be appreciated, its physical properties experienced without contamination by the human element. Zlatni Rat looked better than I had expected, more than what I remembered. I wasn't experiencing the loss of the creature, as Walker Percy described it, I was rediscovering it. And so I felt that even though I was high above Zlatni Rat, I was really on it, or inside it, inside the trueness of it.

I got into my car and headed to the beach. The road eventually led me to Gornji Humac, which was asleep when I arrived—not a soul on its narrow streets, no voices from any of the windows. Even the restaurant, which was open for business, was empty, though there were still glowing embers on the stone slab of the oven. I ate at a gostionica down the highway, sitting on a terrace under a roof of dried palms and by a pool where thatches of lavender grew, and where bees and wasps droned. A mule stood sleepily in the shade of a field behind. On leaving, I tossed him an apple, which he grabbed with his big yellow teeth.

I drove on. I passed an enormous vineyard that went from the road to the summit of the hill, and then I descended sharp switchbacks until I reached Bol.

Bol is a small quaint fishing town on a little harbour facing west where boats are packed at the head and where ice cream stands, cafés and restaurants are packed with customers. In the evenings people sit there and watch the last rays of the sun sloping across the Hvar Channel.

I walked to the head of the harbour and then back again through the pine woods that surround Zlatni Rat.

The Yugoslav-era hotel where we stayed in 1977 was still there, minus the picture of Tito. Sunlight slanted through the forest onto the brown pine-needled floor and the smell of the trees surrounded me. The laughter of kids playing on a bright yellow plastic network of slides and rafts rose from the water. Music, a hum of voices, more muted, came from farther off.

Zlatni Rat was below me. After all these years.

It curled to the right—a cream-coloured peninsula of stone shingles a few hundred metres long with a bright turquoise sea right around its sides and blue Hvar in the distance. A hot, tanned nude woman lay on the right, and another woman rose statuesquely out of the water like Ursula Andress without her white bathing suit and shells. On the beach now, I walked to its head. Tourists had gathered along both edges of the beach where it sloped to the water, but there was still room to lie down. Stone shingles crackled under my sandals. There were no cigarette butts or pieces of garbage on the clean white stones. At the tip of Zlatni Rat I lay down, twisting my back into the pebbles to create a hollow. The point of Zlatni Rat curved slightly to the right, but the form it took today might be different tomorrow because it was always changing, the sea constantly reshaping it. For a time, I don't know how long, I lay there in a fjaka, drowsily hearing voices of Czechs and Hungarians and listening to the hiss of small waves on the pebbles and feeling the sun on my body. Later, I got up and walked down the slope to the water, the stones shifting and sinking under my feet, hard under my soles, and I slipped into the green water that was cool and fresh on my hot skin. Then I swam out towards the blue. Below were schools of small silver fish with black bands around the base of their tails like bowties, and then there was only deepening water. I swam farther out where the sea turned dark. A hundred metres out, the channel pushed strongly towards Bol. There at the edge of the blue current I looked at the island, at the rocky crest of Vidova Gora where I had stood earlier, the wide slopes of dry dark green vegetation through which the road cut like an incision, the town of Bol on my right, with its orange-tiled roofs and harbour of white boats—all of which reminded me of some other town I had already seen, a town that was familiar because of its design, like a morphological pattern in a tale I had grown used to, but a town that became new all over again since I had come to it from a different angle, through a new experience, and saw it fresh all over again. I hung there for a time hardly moving, floating, treading slowly on the channel. I was inside myself and I was looking at the scene. Then I left myself and became part of the scene around me, the blue water and bright light and the pleasant warm wind. It was a moment when I felt happy to be alive.

FIGURE 27. View of Zlatni Rat from Vidova Gora

Return

I returned to the north on the Magistrala. The Adriatic with its white islands was to my left, the Velebit Mountains reared up on my right. When I saw the island of Pag, I felt a twinge of nostalgia for my trips there, for my walk in the heat in the spring of 1996 when I'd trudged alone down this highway heading south. I was tempted to take the exit and cross the bridge to the island. But I continued north.

As I approached the turn up into the Velebits, knowing I was leaving the Adriatic, and soon would enter northern Croatia, I thought of all the people, the thousands who had left their islands behind and had followed this road or a similar one, if they didn't leave by sea. Every departure by land meant crossing these mountains. This moment, when they crested the last peak, when they looked back one last time, if they were able to do so, must have stung them with feelings of sadness and worry, but also filled them with hope. Memories of their leaving, myriad and fresh, just a few hours back there, must have haunted these emigrants now that they were separated from their families, now that they knew, if they ever came back, that neither they nor their islands would ever be the same.

I didn't have these feelings, obviously, when I got to Senj and began the ascent. Instead, I was ready to leave the austere terrain of the islands behind for the green, lush summer countryside of Prigorje. It was a familiar world. I had family and friends there, a history. I felt like I was going home.

I drove up switchbacks as the temperature began to drop. The computer on my rented car showed snowflakes, seemingly a crazy malfunction, until I hit the peak and real flakes began to fall from a leaden sky. They whipped across the windshield for a few minutes until the temperature climbed again and they disappeared. A cool, grey day greeted me on the other side of the mountains. I left behind the last crags and stones poking from dry grassy fields, and I entered a region of cornfields and wheat, of villages clustered in the valleys below rising hills, of vineyards aligned in long straight rows.

I turned in at Jastrebarsko. The main drag passed between rows of buildings on either side, where storks roosted in big nests on chimneys. Soon after, the road led me down through a forest of beach and oak until a gostionica showed up on the right. It had become a tradition of mine to stop here after a trip to the coast before heading home.

I see myself here with my father and son. It is early evening when we get out of the car, and the big iron barbecue is cooling down. On the terrace under a roof supported by heavy wooden beams, we sit at a large wooden table. Grapes grow along the sides and a few stray chickens wander about. Crickets chirp all around us. They aren't the same loud clacking cicadas of the south. The air smells richly of grass and flowers. We look over our menus, check the price of beer. I tell my son, Lucas, that he should drink juice or milk, rather than pop. "It's what your mother would want," I add. "Mom's not here, dad," he answers, and orders a Coke. Joe snaps his menu shut and says, "Well I know what I'm having. And you know what else?" he asks. "What's that?" I wonder. "I'm the pensioner and you're the rich man, a professor, so you're paying, ha-ha," and he lets go that cackle of his. "We'll see," I say.

So we eat our platter of roast pork and roasted potatoes and mixed salad, and Joe and I drink our Ožujsko, fifteen kuna a bottle, and we talk about this and that, Joe giving Lucas advice about his future, his future work life, "You don't want to work with a shovel all your life, do you?" And Lucas answering, as he reaches for his Coke, which he is nursing as he eats, "No, yes, sure, whatever." Then our meal is over. Once we are done, I go inside, take out my credit card and pay. We get into the car and drive the last few kilometrers through winding villages and fields of corn, which seem taller since our trip south, and finally we drive into the valley of Srebrnjak.

Works Cited

Antić, Josip. "The Continuous Brač Wall." In *The Island of Brač*, 112. Translated by Mark Davies et al. Zagreb: Fabro Press, 2006.

Božanić, Joško. "Terra Marique." In *The Adriatic Archipelago Telling Tales*, 119–23 Translated by Stipe Grgas. Split: Hydrographic Institute of the Republic of Croatia, 2010.

Burke, Edmund. *A Philosophical Enquiry into the Origin of Our Ideas of the Sublime and Beautiful*. Oxford: Oxford University Press, 2015.

Chard, Chloe. *Pleasure and Guilt on the Grand Tour: Travel Writing and Imaginative Geography 1600–1830*. Manchester: Manchester University Press, 1999.

Dolenc, Mate. "The Island of Wine and Submarine Caves." In *The Island of Vis*, 82–93. Translated by Janko Paravić. Zagreb: Fabra, 2004.

Fiamengo, Jakša. "The Fjaka, As a Specific State of Mind and Body." *Crown Croatian World Network*. http://www.croatia.org/crown/articles/9842/1/Fjaka---Between-Times.html.

Fiamengo, Jakša. "The Metropolis of Croatian Fishermen." In *The Island of Vis*, 36–47. Translated by Janko Paravić. Zagreb: Fabra 2004.

Hektorović, Petar. *Fishing and Fishermen's Conversation*. Translated by E.D. Goy. *British-Croatia Review* 15 (January 1979): 13–45.

Matvejević, Predrag. *Mediterranean: A Cultural Landscape*. Translated by Michael Henry Heim. Berkeley: University of California Press 1999.

Miller, Henry. *Black Spring*. New York: Grove Press, 1963.

Novak, Slobodan. "Introspective Mirror." In *The Adriatic Archipelago Telling Tales*, edited by Mirjana Tepšić, translated by Stipe Grgas, 127–29. Split: Hydrographic Institute of the Republic of Croatia, 2010.

Percy, Walker. *The Message in the Bottle*. New York: Picador, 1975.

West, Rebecca. *Black Lamb and Grey Falcon: A Journey Through Yugoslavia*. New York: Viking Press, 1941.

Zentz, Wendy. "Yugoslavs Claim Bit of White House." *South Florida Sun Sentinel*, 8 November 1986. http://articles.sun-sentinel.com/1986-11-09/features/8603090262_1_white-house-brac-stone.